LOWELL ARMS.

THE SEMI-CENTENNIAL OF LOWELL.

PROCEEDINGS

IN THE CITY OF LOWELL

AT THE

Semi-Centennial Celebration

OF THE

INCORPORATION

OF THE

TOWN OF LOWELL,

March 1st, 1876.

LOWELL, MASS.:
PENHALLOW PRINTING ESTABLISHMENT, NO. 12 MIDDLE STREET.
1876.

PREFATORY.

The public commemoration of the incorporation of the town of Lowell was first proposed in the Common Council, February 9th, 1875, when Councilman CHARLES COWLEY introduced the following order, which passed both branches of the City Council unanimously:—

"ORDERED, that a joint special committee, to consist of the Mayor, the President of the Common Council, two members of the Board of Aldermen and three members of the Common Council, be appointed to consider the propriety of commemorating the entry of the municipality of Lowell upon the fiftieth year of its existence, on the first day of March next, and to report in what manner, if any, the same should be commemorated."

The Committee appointed under this resolution consisted of Mayor FRANCIS JEWETT, Aldermen JOHN A. GOODWIN and HAPGOOD WRIGHT, ALBERT A. HAGGETT, President, and CHARLES COWLEY, CHARLES W. SLEEPER, and EDWARD E. REED, members of the Common Council. Preparations were begun for the celebration, and the late TAPPAN WENTWORTH was selected as Orator of the Day; but he was called away by death before the time arrived for what would have been to him, as well as to his audience, a most acceptable service.

On account of the lack of time to complete the desired arrangements, the Committee reported the commemoration to be inexpedient until another year. In their report they say:

" Between the appointment of your Committee and the first day of March next, the first day of Lowell's year of Jubilee, there was found

PREFATORY.

to be too little time to make the necessary preparations for such a celebration as the occasion seemed to require. In modern times, the celebration of centennial and semi-centennial anniversaries has, to a great extent, superseded the festivities of the jubilees of ancient times. Your Committee believe that a public commemoration of the founding of our municipality would tend strongly to foster, in the hearts of all our people, an honorable pride in her institutions, her industries, and her history, and a laudable ambition to increase her fair renown;—and that such a celebration should be had while some of those who were present at our municipal nativity, still survive to participate therein; but your Committee deem it advisable, under all the circumstances, to postpone such celebration till the completion of the year of our Jubilee, upon which we are about to enter."

On November 23rd, 1875, the Old Residents' Historical Association sent to the City Council the following communication.

" *To the Mayor, Aldermen and Common Council of the City of Lowell:*

At the Quarterly meeting of the Old Residents' Historical Association, holden Thursday evening, Nov. 11, 1875, it was unanimously

RESOLVED, That this Association earnestly desires that there be a public celebration of the fiftieth anniversary of the municipal independence of the Town, now City, of Lowell, which occurs March 1, 1876; and will gladly co-operate with the City Council in any measures which they may adopt for that purpose.

ALFRED GILMAN,

Secretary."

This communication was referred to a special committee consisting of Aldermen JOHN A. GOODWIN and HAPGOOD WRIGHT, and Councilmen CHARLES COWLEY, W. A. READ and FRANCIS CARLL. Before the expiration of the year, they reported a recommendation that such a celebration be held, and also recommended that the matter be referred to the incoming city government, which suggestion was adopted.

SEMI-CENTENNIAL OF LOWELL.

At the organization of the City Council, January 3rd, 1876, the celebration of this semi-centennial anniversary was recommended by Mayor CHARLES A. STOTT, in his inaugural address. On the same day, the following resolution, introduced by Councilman CHARLES COWLEY, was unanimously adopted:

"RESOLVED, That a joint special committee, to consist of three members of the Common Council and two members of the Board of Aldermen, be appointed to make all necessary arrangements for the public celebration of the fiftieth anniversary of the incorporation of the town of Lowell, March 1st, 1876, and that all papers referred to the present City Council by the last City Council, relating to the commemoration of said incorporation, and also so much of the Mayor's inaugural address as relates thereto, be referred to said committee."

The Committee appointed under this resolution consisted of Councilmen CHARLES COWLEY, JOHN F. KIMBALL and EDWARD STOCKMAN, and Aldermen JOHN A. GOODWIN and GEORGE E. STANLEY.

The following resolution was reported by this Committee, and adopted by the City Council, January 11th.

"RESOLVED, That in commemoration of the incorporation of the town of Lowell, the Mayor, the City Council and the citizens generally, or so many of them as may be pleased so to do, shall assemble in Huntington Hall at two o'clock p. m. on the first day of March next ensuing, being the fiftieth anniversary of said incorporation, for thanksgiving and prayer—for singing in which the children and youth of the public schools shall join—for hearing historical addresses and letters—and for such other exercises as are appropriate to the occasion; and the Mayor shall be requested to preside. From sunrise to sunset, on that day, the American ensign shall be displayed on the public buildings and such other places as the Mayor may direct. At meridian, on said day, a national salute shall be fired, and from meridian to one o'clock the bells shall be rung. The people of the city in general—the survivors of the earlier inhabitants and the Old Resident's Historical Association in particular—are invited to assist in these commemorative services.

The committee of arrangements shall cause a record of said services to be published in a style uniform with other city documents, and the expenses thereof shall be charged to the reserved fund."

The committee of arrangements for the celebration, consisting of JOSIAH G. PEABODY, JOHN W. SMITH, ALFRED GILMAN, BENJAMIN WALKER and HAPGOOD WRIGHT, of the Old Residents' Historical Association, besides the members of the City Council above named, organized by the choice of CHARLES COWLEY as Chairman and JOHN F. KIMBALL as Secretary. Subsequently, the Chairman, Secretary and Alderman GOODWIN were appointed a Committee to superintend the publication of the record of the proceedings.

This Committee met many times; the Mayor and Dr. JOHN O. GREEN, President of the Old Residents' Historical Association, met by invitation with them, and assisted in perfecting the arrangements according to the following revised programme, for a celebration in three distinct parts—forenoon, afternoon, and evening.

Morning Celebration.
1826--1876.

Order of Exercises

AT THE

Semi-Centennial Celebration

OF THE

City of  Lowell,

At Huntington Hall, on Wednesday, March 1st, 1876,

COMMENCING AT 9¼ O'CLOCK.

SINGING BY A CHOIR OF
FIVE HUNDRED PUPILS,
From the Public Schools, assisted by the

Germania Orchestra, of Boston,

GEO. F. WILLEY, Conductor.

PROGRAMME.

1—MARCH, "Athalia," - - - - - *Mendelssohn*
    ORCHESTRA.

2— { (a)—CHORAL, Praise ye the Lord, - *Arranged by Dr. Marx*
     (b)—DOXOLOGY, Mighty God,
    HIGH AND GRAMMAR SCHOOLS.

3—PRAYER,
    By REV. GEORGE F. STANTON, South Weymouth, Mass.

4—GLEE, { (a)—How can I Serve my Country Best? - *A. Freuh*
     (b)—We are Brothers, - - - - *Eskel*
    HIGH SCHOOL.

5—OVERTURE, "Der Freischütz," - - - - - *Weber*
    ORCHESTRA.

6—SONG, (a)—Song of Praise,
   GLEE, (b)—Murmur, Gentle Lyre,
    GRAMMAR SCHOOLS.

7—GLEE, High School March, - - - - *G. A. Veasie*
    HIGH SCHOOL.

8—ADDRESS,
    By REV. WARREN H. CUDWORTH, BOSTON

9—SYLPHIDEN POLKA, (For two Piccolos,) - - - *Rietzel*
    MESSRS. GOERING & RIETZEL.

10—GLEE, The Mermaid's Song, - - - - *S. Glover*
    GRAMMAR SCHOOLS.

11—GLEE, Thy Flow'ry Banks, O lovely River, - *Mayerbeer*
    HIGH SCHOOL.

12 ADDRESS,
    By JONATHAN KIMBALL, Supt. Public Schools, Chelsea, Mass.

13—GLEE, { (a)—See the Setting Sun,
     (b)—Shades of Evening,
    GRAMMAR SCHOOLS.

14—GLEE, { (a)—Hail, Columbia,
     (b)—American Hymn, - - - - *Keller*
    HIGH AND GRAMMAR SCHOOLS.

AFTERNOON CELEBRATION.

1826--1876.

ORDER OF EXERCISES

AT THE

Semi-Centennial Celebration

OF THE

City of Lowell,

AT HUNTINGTON HALL,

WEDNESDAY, MARCH 1st, 1876,

Commencing at 1 o'clock.

MUSIC BY THE

LOWELL CHORAL SOCIETY,

GERMANIA ORCHESTRA,

OF BOSTON.

CARL ZERRAHN, Conductor.

PROGRAMME.

1. OVERTURE, "Raymond." - - - - - AMBROISE THOMAS.
   GERMANIA ORCHESTRA.
2. PRAYER, - - - - - - - - - - - -
   By REV. THEODORE EDSON, S. T. D., CHAPLAIN OF THE DAY.
3. CHORAL, "To God on high." - - - - - MENDELSSOHN.
   From "St. Paul."
   LOWELL CHORAL SOCIETY.
4. ORATION, - - - - - - - - - - - -
   By MAJOR-GENERAL BENJAMIN F. BUTLER.
5. ODE, - - - - - - - - - - - - -
   By JOHN F. FRYE.

TO THE MUSIC OF "KELLER'S AMERICAN HYMN."

Home of the hillside, the torrent, the stream,
Where the wild waters in harmony blend,
How thy waste places with opulence teem!
Tides from their channels submissively bend!
   Tides from their channels, etc.
Here in thy beautiful valleys, 'twould seem,
Nature to Art all her treasures would lend.
   Nature to Art, etc.

Home of our fathers! for toils and for cares,
Came they from mountain and prairie and sea,
Now to the shrine of their faith and their prayers
Come their thinned ranks to thy great jubilee.
   Come their thinned ranks, etc.
Each to thine altar his offering bears,
Temple of Labor, proud boast of the Free!
   Temple of Labor, etc.

Home of their children! the sons of such sires
Guard well thy fame both in peace and in war.
Naught shall e'er quench on thy hearth-stone
   the fires;
Firm we will stand for Truth, Justice and Law,
Cherish thee ever, where'er we may be.
Triumph of Labor, proud boast of the Free,
Come we from mountain and prairie and sea!
Come, one and all, to thy great jubilee!

SEMI-CENTENNIAL OF LOWELL. 13

6. ADDRESSES, - - - - - - - - - - -
By Hon. JOHN A. LOWELL,   Rt. Rev. THOMAS M. CLARK, D. D.,
Hon. MARSHALL P. WILDER, and Rev. A. A. MINER, D. D.,
Alternating with Instrumental Music.

7. CHORUS, "The Heavens are telling." - - - - - - HAYDN.
From the "Creation."
LOWELL CHORAL SOCIETY.

8. HISTORICAL REMINISCENCES, - - - - - - -
By Dr. JOHN O. GREEN, PRESIDENT OF OLD RESIDENTS' ASSOCIATION.

9. HALLELUJAH CHORUS, - - - - - - - - HANDEL.
From the "Messiah."
LOWELL CHORAL SOCIETY.

10. LETTERS, - - - - - - - - - - - -
By Hon. JOSIAH G. ABBOTT, Hon. SETH AMES, SAMUEL BATCHELDER,
and others.

11. POEM, - - - - - - - - - - - - -
By JOHN S. COLBY.

12. OLD HUNDRED, - - - - - - - - - LUTHER.
LOWELL CHORAL SOCIETY, and audience.

From all that dwell below the skies,   Eternal are thy mercies, Lord,
Let the Creator's praise arise;   And truth eternal is thy word :
Jehovah's glorious name be sung   Thy praise shall sound from shore to shore,
Through every land, by every tongue.   Till suns shall rise and set no more.

13. BENEDICTION, - - - - - - - - - -
BY THE CHAPLAIN.

A SOCIAL LEVEE

For the reception of invited guests, and others, at HUNTINGTON HALL
in the evening, at 7½ o'clock.

MUSIC BY THE

GERMANIA BAND.

The national salute ordered by the City Council, was fired by a detatchment of the City Guards on the South Common, between twelve and one o'clock, the bells of the city joining with the guns in celebrating the festival.

Although the weather was unpropitious in the forenoon, the attendance at all the services was very large, exceeding the capacity of Huntington Hall. By general consent, the day was observed as a holiday. All the schools, the banks, and most places of business, were closed, though the mills ran as usual. The presence of hundreds of former residents of Lowell gave peculiar interest to the occasion. The satisfaction of the people with the celebration, in all its parts, seemed to be universal.

The hall was appropriately decorated for the occasion. On the wall in rear of the stage was the inscription, in elegant design, "Semi-Centennial" and below it a field of blue, on canvas. Suspended over the front of the stage was an ornamental device bearing the word, "Lowell," capped with the figures "1876," and below it, on either side, the figures, "1826," and "1836." Surmounting this device was an eagle. From the centre of the ceiling streamers of red, white and blue radiated to different portions of the hall, forming a canopy of the national colors. Flags of all nations were displayed, one from each of the iron posts in the gallery. On the gallery front were the words "Chelmsford," "Dracut" "Tewksbury," and the three towns from which the present territory of Lowell was taken. On the northerly wall was the inscription " Liberty and Union, now and forever; one and inseparable. 1776-1876."

JAMES M. W. YERRINGTON, of Chelsea, reported phonographically the addresses of Mr. CUDWORTH, Mr. KIMBALL, Mr. LOWELL, BISHOP CLARK, Mr. WILDER and Dr. MINER, together with the introductory remarks of the President. The oration of GENERAL BUTLER and the address of Dr. GREEN were delivered from printed slips, and are here reproduced in their order precisely as they were spoken. The other discourses are printed as revised by the respective speakers from Mr. YERRINGTON's notes.

At the annual meeting of the Old Residents' Historical Association, on May 2d, the venerable President of that body thus referred to these commemorative services:—

"But the crowning event of the year has been the Semi-Centennial Celebration. At our meeting last November, the approach of the event was announced and a resolution introduced, passed and sent to the City Council, expressing our earnest wish for a suitable observance of the day. It met with a gratifying reception, and a joint committee of the Council and the Association addressed themselves with extraordinary zeal, judgment and perseverance to perfecting arrangements in great detail for the day. Few persons are aware of the importance and labor of such undertakings. While all classes of the community seemed to be aroused, the "Old Residents" evidently regarded it as their last opportunity. The sight of hundreds of their grey heads, as viewed from the galleries in the hall, is described as singularly impressive. Our large and beautiful hall was densely packed, and hundreds were unable to gain admittance.

We were singularly fortunate in our dignified and graceful president of the day, in the appropriate and exhilarating character of our choral music, in the almost world-wide fame of the semi-centennial orator, in our distinguished guests from abroad, and cheered with the happy greetings of former friends who came long journeys to grace our jubilee. The day realized the era of good feelings and left behind it no causes of regret for omissions or mistakes, and the forthcoming history of it, to be published by the city, will commemorate to distant ages one of the most successful and happy ceremonies it has ever undertaken. In this connection, I may add that eleven odes and poems were sent to your committee, from which selection was made."

MORNING DISCOURSES.

The President.—Ladies and Gentlemen, and Scholars of the Lowell Schools :—To have all song and not some praise, perhaps, would weary you; and therefore your committee considered that it would be instructive as well as entertaining to the scholars of our Lowell schools to hear from one who formerly lived in our midst and attended our schools. I have therefore the pleasure of introducing to you the REV. WARREN H. CUDWORTH, of Boston, formerly a Lowell boy.

ADDRESS
BY REV. WARREN H. CUDWORTH.

Mr. Mayor, Ladies and Gentlemen and Young Friends.—You have been breathing an atmosphere of music and patriotic delight for I do not know how long. I only say and think—unfortunate is the man who was not born in Lowell, as I was, or Chelmsford. That tells you how old I am. It is not, you know, "once an acorn, always an acorn," but "once an acorn, some time an oak;" for this principle of growth, which we have seen so grandly illustrated in the rise, progress and prosperity of Lowell, is a principle that you have only to put into the right conditions immediately to see wonderful and delightful results. It seems hardly credible, as I look around this audience this morning and am assured by those figures ["1826–1876"] that fifty years ago today this place was a kind of swamp or an open field, and of the thousands and tens of thousands that now occupy the area of comfortable homes, happy firesides and crowded school rooms in Lowell, only a few hundred then existed, and they had undertaken a task in regard to which there was a great deal of uncertainty, and a great many people were ready and willing to say, "There is no money in that; no success in that." It seems hardly credible that such was the case; yet it was verily the case in the history of our city. But the principle of growth has been applied to this city; its conditions have been industriously and faithfully fulfilled, and behold the result! The principle of growth always vindicates itself when its conditions are wisely, properly and thoroughly fulfilled.

There is the little cotton ball that you take from the Southern field, and you put it at first into the gin, and separate the seed from it; and you get all the masses of the fleecy wealth of the South and bind them into bales, and they are brought here to Lowell. Is that the end of it? Why it is only the beginning of it. It is just with this raw material as it is with the raw materials upon the galleries and behind me,—and pretty raw some of it is, I should judge, by these cat-calls. You take those bales of cotton into your mills, but the cotton is not at once transformed into cloth, to produce the wealth that has made this city of comfortable homes, and instructed and brought up so many delightful people,—for everybody who lives in Lowell is delightful. After the bale is unpacked, the cotton is first carried to the picker-room; and any one who has ever been in a picker-room knows what sort of a place it is. I have been there, and rejoice to say it, to-day. There it is torn into shreds piled up in fleecy masses. In this dusty, noisy place men used to work twelve, fourteen, sixteen hours a day. Have you not made some progress, Lowell men? I think you have come down to eight hours a day; but that, I believe, is the result of necessity, not of any preference on the part of the men who own the mills. At any rate, there is the cotton. That is not the end of it, as you know, it has to be drawn through those torturing cards, and there it is again attacked by ten hundred thousand, or I do not know how many, little teeth, that tear it and pull it and throw it into little masses, and then, you know, it goes into the spinning frame, where it is whirled and whirled until at last it is twisted into threads; and then it is carried into the dressing room, and there subjected to processes which are indispensable; and then it is carried to the weaving room, and there the shuttle flies to and fro, preparing it for use; and at last, after it has been through the examiner's hands, it is sent away from Lowell to Boston, or some other great center of commerce, where it is disposed of, and you can buy it for five, six, or ten cents a yard. But all these processes have to be gone through with this raw material, and it re-appears in I will not undertake to say how many shapes in this audience to-day, and all over the city, the state, the country, the world. It re-appears in the completed and perfected article, after it has been subjected to all those torturing and tormenting processes.

So it is with that wisp of wool, which you would hardly pick up in the street, it is so discolored, so tangled, and in such a snarl. And yet there are people who live on the corporation over yonder, who pick up just such tangles and snarls, and some how or other after subjecting them to various processes, they re-appear in this bunting, and re-appear in the clothing that covers us Just so it is with young persons. Just so it is with the wood of the forest. So it is with the metal in the mine. So it is with the stone or marble in the quarry. God does not give us perfected materials, he gives us raw materials. He gives us little children, that do not know anything, and your Lowell men take them into your schools; they go through the primary school to the grammar school, and from the grammar school to the high school, and before they get through there, they are prepared to delight us with just such music as we have heard to-day.

I suppose that a great deal of the credit is due to these Germanians, or to Mr. Willey, the conductor. At any rate, it has been a noble performance, so far. Perhaps these singers will break down before the end, but I do not think they will. It is not the habit of the boys and girls of Lowell to break down. Whatever they say they will do, they are pretty sure to accomplish.

I believe it is just as natural to prosper and succeed in this world as it is to walk or breathe. God gives us the raw material in the mine to work up into machinery that shall transform the cotton from the field and the wool from the back of sheep into cloth and bunting, and all that makes life delightful, ornate and desirable; and God gives us our nature in the raw material (and very raw sometimes it is), in order that we may work it up into something that is shapely, serviceable, enjoyable, and delightful. And so I say, it is just as natural to prosper and succeed in this world, if you will only grow and fulfil the conditions of growth, as it is to walk or breathe.

I remember reading once of a clergyman who used to preach "decrees," in a way so positive that his wife considered him to be almost a fatalist. He was always saying, "It is decreed so and so, and so it must be." One day when he was about leaving home to fulfil a frontier missionary engagement, knowing that he must pass through a forest that was infested with Indians, he took his rifle down from its supports, and put it into unusually good order. His wife, observing this, thought her opportunity had come to rally him upon his inconsistency. " My dear," says she, " why do you take down your rifle, and put it into unusually good order? you are all the time preaching *decrees*. Now if it is decreed that you will be shot, that rifle won't prevent it; and if it is not decreed that you shall be shot, you don't need that rifle. So why do you take it any way." She thought she had him, but she found he had her,—and that is generally the case. For he at once replied—" My dear, I understand ; I see it all ; but suppose when I went through the forest, I should meet an Indian, and his time had come, and I had not got any rifle, why what on earth would the poor fellow do? You see, my dear, we must do our part towards fulfilling the decrees of Providence ! "

That is the doctrine I want to teach you, my young friends. I was a little child, like the boys and girls here, I won't tell how many years ago. I went through the Primary school in Lowell, I went through the Grammar school in Lowell, under Mr. Graves, I went to the High school, and from there to Phillip's Academy, and then to Harvard College and the Divinity School. I know all about the boys and girls of Lowell, and other places, too, and what I want to impress upon you is, that it is the will of God that you shall succeed and prosper in this world. It is his desire that you should do something in this world to make it and to leave it a great deal better than you found it; and you can do so if you only think so, if you only make up your minds to fulfil the pre-requisite conditions. But you must fulfil those conditions, which are these : that you must trust God; that you must be true; that you must stand immoveably upon the rock of principle; that you must live for the higher ends of your being. Then you will prosper, then you will succeed.

Three men took a job for four dollars, and the question was how to divide the money among them so as to make it equal. There is a problem for the boys and girls in arithmetic. Two of the men discussed it *pro* and *con* a long time. The other said nothing at all, —and at last, and that is generally the case, " for speech may be silvern, but silence is always golden"—they deferred to him, because he had said nothing, and asked him his opinion as to how they could make a division. He replied at once, for he had been watching for just that opportunity. " It is simple enough—there are two dollars for you two, and here are two dollars for me, too." That was his arithmetic. Well, that is the arithmetic of a great many people in this world.

and I assure you they never prosper. They may amass wealth; they may gain fame; they may for awhile seem to be the lions of their day; but, public opinion, sooner or later, finds out the man that makes it two dollars for himself when he is taking in money, and only one or less than one when he is paying away any, and very soon the lion is dismissed with a kick.

Ambitious boys who feel disposed to repine over the obstacles they have to surmount ere they rise in the world, should remember this—those obstacles are just what you need; they constitute a kind of divine spur to progress, so that under the influence of that spur you will be able to progress a great deal further and faster than you would if you were constanly helped by somebody else. There was a boy, who, at the age of ten, was apprentice to a farmer and served out his time of apprenticeship. At the end of eleven years of labor, he received one yoke of oxen and six sheep, which he sold for eighty-eight dollars. That boy did not spend one hundred dollars for himself from the time he was born until he was twenty-one years of age. His name was Henry Wilson, and he became the Vice President of the United States. If it had not been for the obstacles that Henry Wilson had to encounter and surmount, he never would have accomplished the glorious work he did. Ambitious boys, think of that!

And I am not going to forget you, girls. I cannot forget you, because I recall the history of Phœbe and Alice Carey, the daughters of a poor farmer in Central New York, who resolved that, in spite of the narrow circumstances in which they were bound, they would do something grand and noble for humanity. They were compelled to melt lard, which they got from the farm, for oil, and they put into it strips of rags for a wick, to furnish light. That is a lamp to write poetry by! Yet they did write poetry, and true poetry, too, for they put their hearts and souls into every line they wrote. The first six months they got only ten dollars from Mr. Bailey, of the "National Era," a paper then published in Washington. Ten dollars for six months labor! But they kept on. They were resolved not to be intimidated by their narrow circumstances, that they would persevere, and carry out their high purpose; and they have left poetry which will live as long as this English language of ours shall be spoken, and I calculate (I have a right to say this to day) that that language will be spoken as long as the world stands. Indeed, I am inclined to think that it will be, finally, the universal language. I say this, of course, with all deference to my German friends who are around and behind me. But that is what Phœbe and Alice Cary did, notwithstanding the narrow circumstances, in which they were born. So they fulfilled the requisite conditions of success.

How many a Lowell name comes up to me at this time? First, I recall John Neal, the painter. Raw material was he, when he first began to think that he would try to draw, and then that he would try to color. I suppose that if John Neal lives long enough, he will be one of the greatest painters in the world. A Lowell boy, starting as raw material, and going on and on, in accordance with the principle of growth to which I have referred, until he illustrates the law of progress in the department to which he has devoted himself, as Lowell illustrates it in the domain of industry, and will illustrate it in the domain of art by and by.

Then there is Rev. Dr. Huntington, son of Dr. Huntington, for whom this hall is reared, and your former Mayor, whom so many before me knew well as a little boy in school. Then there is Dr. John C. Dalton, whose books on medicine, hygiene and physiology it is a perfect delight to any educated man or woman to read. Then there was Gustavus V. Fox, Assistant Secretary of the Navy, and another who went out as a colonel from New Hampshire, and came back as a general. And let me speak with the deepest feeling and with the profoundest reverence of those two sons of Judge Abbott, noble young men, who would have made their mark in any society, who, when that flag needed defenders, buckled on the armor of the soldier, *and gave their lives, with hundreds of Lowell men, without whose valor, intrepidity, and devotion this hall might not have been thronged to-day, as, thank God, it is because they were devoted and patriotic, and did their duty at the cost of their lives. Every Lowell boy I saw, whether in my own regiment or other regiments, or in the batteries there, I could not help greeting with a warm and friendly grasp of the hand, for I knew what the spirit of the Lowell boys would be, the spirit of Judge Abbott's sons, and other noble and heroic young men, who did their best and gave their best to save the Union from destruction.

I say that all we have to do is to fulfil the conditions of growth, and the Lord will do the rest. I have no doubt there are before me two or three young persons who read a certain large book, and if that is the case, I will ask them to tell me one or two things after I have narrated an incident or two in connection with that book, to illustrate the principle upon which I am dwelling. There was a shepherd, who had a son, and he sent that son into his field to take care of his flocks, and the time passed very heavily on his hands. Those sheep were in a very orderly and proper condition, and what to do to spend the time was the question with him, until at last one day he said, "I will take a sling, and sling stones at a mark." So he took a sling, and began to sling stones at a mark. If you ever did that, you know the first stone you sling almost always goes the other way, because you have to get accustomed to that delicate weapon, and so I suppose it was with that shepherd boy. But at last, persevering, he came nearer and nearer the mark, and that encouraged him, and he kept slinging stones day after day, until finally he could hit the mark every time. He did not know what he was about, but the Lord knew what he was about, for by and by, one of the wars that have existed from the beginning of time broke out between his country and another country, and the armies of the two countries met to settle the trouble by fighting. As they were standing ready for battle, there came out a large fellow, who had a spear like a weaver's beam,—and everybody in Lowell knows how large a weaver's beam is,—and he had on a coat of mail, and a helmet on his head, and sandals on his feet, and a shield so large that it took another man to carry it. He came out and challenged anybody on the other side to come forth and meet him, and he said, " If any one of you whip me, we will be your slaves forever, and if I whip him, you shall be our slaves forever." But the men on the other side shook and trembled with fear, for he was so large, it seemed as if all he had got to do was to put his foot over any one of them, and extinguish him on the spot. But it chanced that the father of this young man came to him one day and said, " My son, I want you to go to the army and carry some loaves that your mother has just baked to your brothers in the army." Every soldier here knows how nice it is to get a loaf of home-made bread in the army, especially after eating hard tack. Well this young man took the loaves of bread, from his mother's oven, and carried them to the army, and while he was there, this large fellow came out, and repeated his challenge, and the men in the army of this young man began to shake and tremble and shrink away as usual. But the shepherd boy rode forward and began to look him over from head to foot; looked up to see what kind of a helmet he had on, and down to see what kind of sandals he had on; and he looked so curious and unterrified, that the people behind began to think, " Perhaps he will fight with him." He did not seem to be frightened at all. So they went and told the king that a young fellow had come out from a sheep field who did not seem to be terrified by the giant, and the king sent for him and he was brought into his tent. The king asked him if he would go and fight the giant. "Yes," he said, without any hesitation whatever, certainly he would go and fight him, and deliver his country from the peril in which it was at that time. So the king put his own armor upon him, put sandals on his feet, and a helmet on his head, and gave him his own sword, and then he said, "It is only the destruction of one man." So he went forth, but he had hardly set his foot out of the king's tent, before he felt very uncomfortable in that coat of mail; he had never worn any such thing in his life before, so he went back into the tent, and asked the king to let him take off the armor, and as for the sword, he said it might snap the moment he struck with it. "I think I have got something," says he, "that will answer." The king said, "yes, I have only to lose one man.' So he took off the coat of mail, and the helmet and the sandals, and bare-headed and bare-footed, with nothing but his shepherd's frock on, and a little bag hung at his side, in which he had put a few smooth stones that he had taken out of the brook, he went out to meet the giant. Do you wonder that when the giant saw him come tripping towards him, and coming nearer and nearer every moment he looked with perfect contempt upon him, and wondered what sort of a phenomenon it was that was coming out to meet him in that way? But as he came nearer, he saw there was mischief in his eye. If you want to know whether a man means mischief or not, look him right square in the eye, you can tell at once, for the eye is the window of the soul. The lips may deceive, the other features may be a sort of mask, but if you look at the eye, if there is mischief there, it will come right out, and call itself by name. So it was with this young man. As he came nearer and nearer to the giant, the giant saw there was mischief in that young fellow, and said to himself, "I guess I must be ready for him." So as he came nearer, he saw him take a little piece of leather, with two strings, out of his script or bag, which was slung a this side, and then he put a small stone into the bit of leather; and he could not help exclaiming in his wrath, "Am I a dog, that you should come out to meet me with stones?" "I will let you know what I have come out to meet you with," says the young man, and immediately slung a stone which struck the giant in the forehead, and he fell to the earth. Then the young man ran up to him and drew his sword out of its scabbard, and cut off his head with his own sword. Who was that young man? [Several voices]—" David." Why, you know all about it! I don't believe one of these old folks could have told me. [Laughter] Now, who was the big fellow? ["Goliah."] I am glad you read your Bibles. Read your Bibles every day. Study them. The Bible is the best book on earth. I know, for I have read a great many books. You may ask good Dea. Knowles, and he will tell you the same. He has been such a good friend of mine that I delight to say it in his presence. You can ask any of the older persons here, and they will say, "Read your Bibles."

Now, here is the point, and I think you will understand it. When David was slinging stones at the mark, he did not know what he was about. But the Lord knew that every time he hit the mark with one of those stones, he was hitting Goliah. And every time, my young friends, that you get your grammar lesson, or drawing lesson, or any of the lessons that are given you in your school perfectly, and recite it well, you are just like David hitting the mark with his stones; and the more you observe the laws of your intellectual nature, the more you will grow in knowledge, and the more you observe the laws that govern moral qualities, the more your moral natures will grow; and at last, when the world comes with its burdens, and these are laid on your shoulders, you will be as ready to discharge your duty and bear those burdens as David was when the Lord put him before Goliah. Although he was bare-headed and barefooted, and had his shepherd's frock on, and nothing but his sling in his hand, and his opponent was armed *cap a pie*,—from head to foot— and wielded a mighty sword, and had a spear like a weaver's beam, yet in a second he was on his back, and his head was off, because David trusted in the Lord, and the lord was with him. If you will observe these principles of growth, in perfect truth, you will find that, sooner or later, they will produce their results.

The celebrated Dean Swift was walking on the Phœnix road one day, when a shower came up, which troubled him very much. At last, he found shelter under a tree, where he found a number of people, in some trepidation and embarrassment. They were much disconcerted because the shower had come up. He saw that one of the girls of the party began to cry, her handkerchief was up to her eyes, and she was sobbing and crying and taking on in a way that awakened his sympathy. So he went up to her and said, " My dear what is the matter?" He found that it was her wedding day, and she had on her wedding dress, and was afraid that the rain would take all the starch out, and then she could not go to church, and then she could not get married, and then she burst into tears afresh. "Never mind," said the good Dean, "I am a clergyman and can marry you just where you are." So he put his hand into his pocket and took out a prayer-book, and then and there, made them man and wife, and to complete the marriage ceremony, he tore a blank leaf out of his prayer-book and wrote and signed, then and there, this unique marriage certificate:

"Under a tree, in stormy weather,
I married this man and woman together;
Let none but him who rules the thunder,
Sever this man and woman asunder."

Well, Dean Swift trusted in Providence, and so he was enabled to accomplish that work; and those people, of course, were a great deal better married, then and there, then they would have been, if they had gone to church, because the Dean did not charge them any fee, and wrote this unique marriage certificate, and enabled me to tell the story here.

Trust, and be true. And, as an illustration of truth, I will tell you a story of a little boy who would always tell the truth, and he was not George Washington, either; but he would always tell the truth, no matter what the occasion might be. He was a very frank, noble, and generous boy. I guess he was born in Lowell. At any rate, he was a delightful boy. A clergyman who had been visiting at the house said to him one day, "I have been very much pleased with you since I have been in your house, and I want to make you a present before I go away. What shall I give you?" The little fellow had a great respect for the cloth, that is, for clergymen,—which is a very proper thing—always respect your minister, children. He had great respect for the cloth, and thought that it would be proper for him to ask for something of a religious character, like a Sunday-school book, or a prayer-book, or a Bible, and so he said, "Well sir, I suppose I ought to ask for a New Testament, but I know I want a squirt-gun." He told the truth, and he got the squirt-gun and the New Testament, too. Now, always tell the truth, always trust in God, always observe these principles of growth in a pure and proper manner, and you will find, when you get to be men and women, and the burdens of mature or later life are put upon you, that you can bear them. If there is any one in this audience who does not believe that, he reminds me of the Irishman's turtle who was dead without knowing it. The Irishman, it seems, had cut off a turtle's head, and was very much astonished to see him wriggling around for several days afterwards, and when he manifested his astonishment by exclaiming, "Sure, and he must be dead, for how could the crathur live without his head?" And his companion said, "Of course he is dead, but the poor crathur isn't sensible of it." Now I say that every one who does not live for the development of himself in the best way, for the good of others, and for

the honor of the infinite Father of us all, is dead without knowing it.
He is dead who does not give his life for others, and live for their
benefit and advantage.

"He is dead whose hand is not opened wide
To help the want of some one or other,
He doubles the good of his life-long ride
Who gives his fortunate place to his brother,
And a thousand million lives are his
Who carries the world in his sympathies.
  To live is to give,
  To deny is to die.

The flower shines not for itself at all,
Its joy is the joy it freely diffuses,
Of beauty and balm it is prodigal,
And it lives in the life it sweetly loses,
No choice for the rose, but glory or doom,
To exhale or smother, to wither or bloom.
  To live is to give,
  To deny is to die.

Forever the sun is pouring his gold
On a hundred worlds that beg and borrow;
His warmth he squanders on summits cold,
His wealth on the houses of want and sorrow;
To deny his largess of precious light
Is to bury himself in eternal night.
  To live is to give,
  To deny is to die.

The sea lends silvery rain to the land,
The land its saphire streams to the ocean;
The heart sends blood to the brain of command;
The brain to the heart its lightning motion;
And ever and ever we yield our breath
Till the mirror is dry, and images death.
  To live is to give,
  To deny is to die.

Throw gold on the far-dispensing wave,
And your ships sail home with tons of treasure,
Care not for comfort, all hardship brave,
And evening and age shall sup with pleasure;
Fling health to the sunshine, breeze and rain,
And roses come back to the cheek again.
  To live is to give,
  To deny is to die."

The President.—Now Ladies and Gentlemen, and Scholars of the Lowell High School, I can remember, when myself perhaps as young as the youngest here, that a gentleman came to me, and, looking down into my face, and putting his hand on my head, said, "Young man, I hope some day that you will give a good account of your time." And I remember my dear mother held up to me, as an example, the gentleman who is now to address you. I cannot introduce him better to you, than in the language of the poet, speaking of the magnificent river that flows along our borders:

"Though deep, yet clear, though gentle, yet not dull,
Strong without rage, without overflowing, full."

ADDRESS
By Jonathan Kimball, Superintendent of Public Schools, Chelsea, Mass.

Ladies and Gentlemen, Citizens of Lowell and Children of the Public Schools.—The vast size of this room, the number of active, lively faces which form its circle, the yet lingering strains of music, as well as these gorgeous decorations above us, significant of the fact, that the nations of the world have their representatives, silent, if not speaking here, remind me, and I suppose remind you, that this is what you might call in Lowell a gala day. It is a gala day when one after long experience in life, comes to celebrate his silver or his golden wedding. It is a gala day when cities, which have a longer being than the inhabitants who compose them, set apart a day to commemorate their birth, and make the most of it as a day of rejoicing.

I am here to-day, at the request of your committee, for the purpose of saying a word on an occasion, which, to me, is one of great pleasure; for, of course, those who have known me formerly, will remember that my life runs back so far as to have ante-dated the birth of this large and prosperous city. I might almost call the Merrimack my native river. I might, perhaps, with propriety, quote the language of Whittier himself, when he speaks of that sweetly flowing stream, "Whose valley the sunset fills," for the first sunset that ever made an impression upon my spirit, was made across the waters of the Merrimack, and the first steps it was my privilege to take upon earth, remembering them, were taken in your streets, by the side of your streams and through your forests, or wending my way, not "like snail, unwillingly to school," but joyfully, eagerly.

But this is not an occasion to indulge at any length in reminiscenses of the past. Here is Lowell; I need not say " Behold her ! Judge for yourselves!" For you old citizens, and you young citizens to come, know Lowell far better than I do or can, or than any of us can that have been exiled any length of time. But here she is, behold her! She owes her success, she owes this great gathering which we have to-day of those called together to commemorate her fiftieth anniversary, to certain facts. First, the fact of situation. There are few cities so favorably located for manufacturing purposes, as it were by the hand of God, as the city of Lowell. She had a history even before the aborigines left her territory, or Chelmsford received its name.

She had the most convenient river of New England; the best waterfall that could be culled out of all its numerous descents; and from the capital which was early attracted here, and the foresight which guided that capital and directed it—as capital, I am sorry to say, is not always directed—to reasonable, just, far sighted and moral ends, she has had a reputation and a history from the begining which have been things to speak about and be proud of, and very few of those drawbacks which belong to some enterprises inagurated and carried on, giving fame or infamy to other places and other cities. I think, as one of the citizens of Lowell, I may say, if you will allow me to call myself a fellow-citizen, that we owe a great deal to this situation and to this employment of capital.

I am reminded that in recent days, capitol and labor have been attempted to be made antagonistic; that there have been "strikes;" that individuals, sometimes forgetting their actual situation, and sometimes attributing motives to others which they would be unwilling to have attributed to themselves, and sometimes, with just reason, having complained of those from whom they received employment, have been so unwise and injudicious as to attempt to set at variance the water and the wheel, and to attempt to produce results by one without the aid of the other.

Lowell, too, has been fortunate in the character of the men who founded it. I have been very much interested in thinking over my boyish reminiscences of the men who started the business of manufacturing in this locality. I can remember, perfectly well, the tall, and stalwart form of Boott, the first citizen of New England at the time, owing to his connection with this growing enterprise. He always climbed the ladders where his men were at work, with his arms at full length, never bending the elbow, holding himself back in such a position that he could see the end from the beginning; and the man who physically sees the end from the beginning, or attempts it, is very likely, mentally and morally, to see the end from the beginning. I do not know whether he did or not, but his foresight and far-reaching vigilance did very much toward the development of this city.

I must not dwell upon these matters of reminiscence; but what is Lowell? Because when an enterprise is created, through agencies of whatever kind, and yet it results in nothing, we are very apt to say, according to the Latin verse,

"*De nihilo nihil, in nihilum nil posse reverti,*"

and when you get nothing out of *much*, the remark is still more forcible. Lowell has something to show. She has her results, and she shows them in the civil institutions which she has reared, under the government of the people, supported by the strength, and buttressed by the intelligence, and made inexpugnable by the will of the people who have founded the constitution under which she has lived. She has had institutions, without which the inhabitants to-day, would not be the inhabitants they are. Early in her history, I can recall very well, without having had any particular familiarity with them, the interest that was evinced by the leading men of the city in those institutions. They have grown like the grain of mustard seed in the Gospel, until they have made this city a mighty tree, bearing fruit every day, and fruits not to be disregarded. She has had industrial institutions that have lined the shores of your rivers with splendid mills, that have driven the fish from your waters, that have leveled hills and filled up valleys, that have gone northward and eastward and southward, until they are the boast of Lowell. Whatever of beauty she possesses from the hand of Nature, whatever attractiveness she presents to coming residents, and to those who shall first see the light within her limits, will be enhanced, further, by civil and religious privileges such as have made her distinguished, and upon which I would gladly enlarge were I not admonished that gratitude has its limits as well as its promptings.

Lastly, and important, among all others she has reared educational institutions, in which I may say, as one of this army of teachers, one having a sympathy with the subject, one knowing many of those who are amongst you, and as one having long been with you, I feel a sincere pride. I love Lowell for her educational institutions. To dwell upon them in detail would be out of place, to dwell upon them in detail would be harassing to your patience; but it is a pleasing thought,—I feel it as an old man, who has been a boy, and has travelled step by step, as my friend who preceded me in speaking has said, through their different grades. I feel a gratitude for them which cannot be expressed in language, cannot be expressed in any form which I can adopt. They have given the children of the past,—inferior, perhaps, as you of the present would consider them,—they have given the children of the past an opportunity of crossing that vast chasm that intervenes between knowledge and ignorance; they have given the children of the past, who otherwise might have wandered in the deserts east of Africa, an oportunity to cross the river and enter the promised land. They have given the children of the past the means of starting at the beginning, and going on to see how much rests in the power of early education. Thanks to the Fathers of the city, thanks to those who early with enlightened minds, saw what a population like this needed, and walking in the light of what they saw, gave us the institutions under which we have grown up, and which have made us, with capital, situation and skill, what we are. They have given us that, for which we have reason to be grateful. I take this opportunity, on the fiftieth anniversary of the City of Lowell, and the year, I believe, which commemorates its fiftieth annual school report, to say that it is this invincible power of education, which grasping the raw material of the human mind, and, step by step, slowly disentangling its crooked natural tendencies, separating out the fibres, which were otherwise rolled together, until they scarcely had form or comliness, has given the communities that have possessed the advantages of that power, an opportunity to stand up and produce the men whom we love and honor.

I am afraid that, with the garrulity of an old teacher, I am talking too long on this matter of education; but it is one that has been near my heart ever since I received some of its advantages, ever since it aided me to speak, think and work, and this tribute is properly its due.

I read last evening a few lines in a book having reference to old cities, and it occurred to me this morning, as I was passing along, to inquire what would be the probable impression that would cross the mind of one who in years to come should view the memorials of this city. A man who to-day stands at the entrance of the Temple of Luxor, in Egypt, runs his eye along an avenue of sphinxes, passes through it, and praises the architect and the power that raised those mighty columns which have been, for so many centuries, the wonder of the world. But when he gets to the end, he finds himself amid a vast idolatrous temple, where heathen gods, "full of rage, revenge and lust," with their stolid faces and gloomy eyes looked down upon imagined worshippers thirty or forty generations ago. Who are to read our ruins? Who are to recall the institutions, and the habits of thought and life of the people who filled the streets of Lowell, its schools and manufactories, for the past fifty years? What will they say of us? How idle it is for us to prophecy; and yet how unwise not to attempt, from our knowledge of the present, to forecast, to some extent, the future. When the column of knowlege is once reared upon the plain of human thought and human affection, when the column of industry is reared there, when the column of virtue is reared there, and when upon these columns you have placed the arch of religion, morality and high purity, you have laid foundations, raised pillars, and built structures destined to be more indestructible than those which, in their ruins, raise such emotions of wonder and awe on the banks of the Euphrates and the Nile. I love to think of Lowell not only as having within itself the elements of those triumphal arches which the people of future times shall read, and *not* wonder to what manner of men they belonged, *not* marvel by what skill they were raised, *not* be astonished at the inscriptions which are to be read upon them. They will read them without the aid of any Champollion to interpret them; they will read them with eyes that belong to intelligent men and women, and will be gratified to say, that whatever changes may have taken place in the institutions of this country, there once dwelt in the angle of the Merrimack a people of high industry and high practical art, who yet never forgot that upon general education depend general morality and general prosperity.

The Chairman of the Committee of Arrangements.—In addition to the two gentlemen who have already spoken, the Committee of Arrangements invited as a third speaker, this morning, the Rev. Dr. Huntington, to whom Mr. Cudworth has alluded, one of the sons of the late Dr. Elisha Huntington, who filled during nine annual terms the office of Mayor of the city of Lowell. Nothing but his supreme regard for his own parish and his parochial duties, (which also led him to decline the mitre which was offered to him, a few months ago, by the Diocese of Iowa,) has prevented him from being with us to-day. His letter in reply to our invitation reads as follows:—

WORCESTER, FEB. 5, 1876.

My Dear Sir:—An imperative engagement obliges me to be at home in Worcester on the first of March. Otherwise nothing would give me greater pleasure than to be at home in Lowell on that day. I beg to thank you and your associates on the Committee for the offered privilege of addressing the children of the schools. That I owe the honor of receiving this appointment to the circumstance of my having been the son of an "old resident," in no degree diminishes my sense of your kindness; for it touches my feelings very deeply to be thus assured that my father's name is still held in affectionate remembrance in the city which it was always his delight to serve.

I have lived now a long while away from Lowell, but nothing shall ever persuade me that anywhere else there are public buildings so imposing, walks and rides so attractive, or river scenery so fine as those to which my childhood was used.

My best wish for the young people now growing up amid all these advantages, is, that they may appreciate them as warmly as I did when I was a boy, and may always feel an honest pride in remembering that they were born within sound of the factory bells.

I am very sincerely and respectfully yours,

WILLIAM R. HUNTINGTON.

TO CHARLES COWLEY, ESQ., *Chairman, etc., etc.*

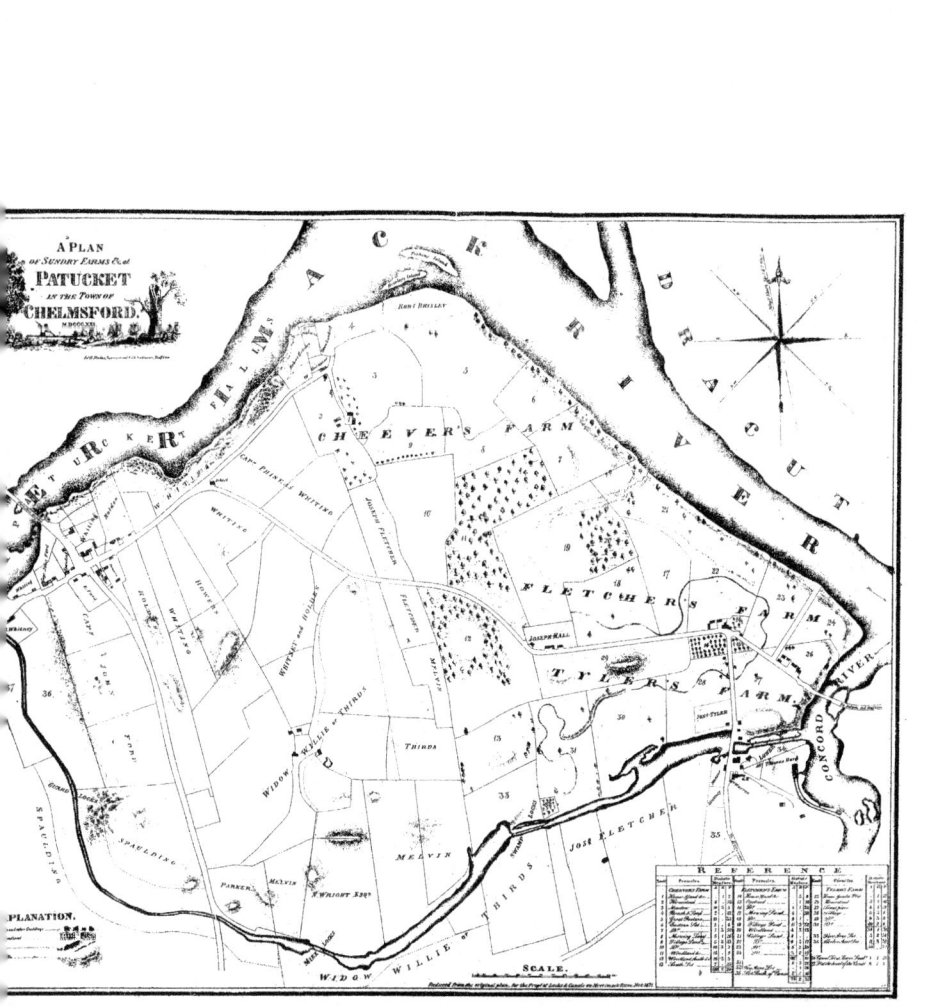

AFTERNOON EXERCISES.

A stirring overture by the Germania Band, of Boston, (twenty-five pieces,) under the leadership of C. H. Eichler, commenced the exercises in the afternoon. The Chairman of the Committee of Arrangements then made the following introductory address.

REMARKS OF CHARLES COWLEY.

Ladies and Gentlemen: On the first day of March, 1826, the act of the General Court incorporating the town of Lowell received the executive approval. At that stroke of Governor Lincoln's pen, Lowell started into municipal life. In view of the approach of this fiftieth anniversary of that event, the City Council, some months ago, resolved to invite the inhabitants of Lowell, past and present, to assemble at this time and place in celebration of the day, and committed to myself and others the duty of making arrangements for proceedings suited to such an occasion. How well this project for commemorative services was received, this thronged audience sufficiently attests. The responses made to the Committee of Arrangements by all whom we have invited to assist in the exercises of to-day, have been most gratifying, indicating that our invitations were regarded as having, (to use the words of General Cushing on another occasion,) "the double force of a command to be obeyed in dutiful gratitude, and of a summons to the enjoyment of exquisite gratification."

It belongs to other tongues than mine to lead your meditations over this retrospect of fifty eventful years; and you have doubtless learned already, from the printed programmes and from the public press, what trained and richly endowed intellects have been secured as contributors to your instruction and enjoyment to-day. I thank them for their readiness to augment the interest of this occasion by contributions from their stores of personal recollections, local traditions, and general knowledge and eloquence. And now, unwilling to detain you with any further introductory remarks, I introduce to you the Hon. Charles A. Stott, Mayor of Lowell, as President of the Day.

ADDRESS OF THE PRESIDENT OF THE DAY.

Ladies and Gentlemen: Fifty years ago the inhabitants of that part of Chelmsford situated at the junction of the Concord with the Merrimack river (and numbering about 2500) finding that they were not being justly dealt with by the mother town, and feeling that their wants would be better cared for under a separate government, petitioned the General Court to be incorporated into a town by the name of Lowell. The prayer of the petitioners was granted and we meet to-day to celebrate by appropriate ceremonies the fiftieth anniversary of that event.

"Invention came with eagle eye,
And science smiled where savage war-fires blazed."

In behalf of the City Council I extend a cordial greeting and welcome to every returning son and daughter of Lowell. Welcome, back to the scenes of your childhood and early life, to join with us in celebrating the semi-centennial of our existence as a town and city. Welcome, you who have lingered by the old hearthstone while others wandered far away. Welcome, you who have from time to time, cast your lot with us although not to the "manor born." Welcome, thrice welcome, all who meet with us to celebrate our natal day, and at the "table of memory to banquet" upon the recollections of the past.

How prophetic the language of the great chief of the Pawtuckets, uttered more than two hundred years ago, when in transferring his authority to his son he exclaimed, "The Great Spirit whispers to me, 'Tell your people peace, peace is the only hope of your race. I have given fire and thunder to the pale-faces as weapons. I have made them plentier than the leaves of the forest, and still they shall increase. These meadows they shall turn with the plough; these forests shall fall by the axe; the pale faces shall live upon your hunting grounds, and make their villages upon your fishing places.'" How fully has this prediction been realized! To-day we are assembled upon what was once their happy hunting grounds; "here the Indian hunter pursued the panting deer; here the council fire glared upon the wise and daring; here they paddled their light canoe along our rocky shore." Not a vestige remains of those who formerly peopled the banks of our beautiful river. Instead of the wigwam with its feeble smoke rise massive structures, busy with the "whirl of spindle and the clack of loom," monuments of man's wise sagacity and untiring perseverance. We meet, my friends, not to listen to elegant and studied oratory, but rather to indulge in reminiscences of the past, full of so much to gladden the heart, and still there comes a feeling of sadness when we look around, and our eye fails to discover the forms of those who were dear to us in our childhood and manhood days.

Where are they? Some in distant lands, some upon the Pacific slope, some in the sunny south, others in the far west, who though not present with us in the flesh, I trust are celebrating this day with us in spirit. But a far greater number have passed on before, and await our coming in the celestial realms above, teaching us the important lesson that life is but the threshold to the tomb.

Oh how pleasant it is to take by the hand those with whom we rambled up and down the banks of our beautiful river and feel the warm pulsation of heart to heart; still more pleasant to meet with those who fashioned the young mind intellectually and morally; they who patiently but kindly watched over us during our school days, ever ready to assist us in our difficult problems, and to make the path to wisdom easy to our feeble steps; and as well those who from week to week directed our thoughts to that better life, and counselled us to walk in the fear of God, and to practice his precepts. To those dear friends of our youth we can only say, God bless you, the seed which you must have thought fell in stony ground, I trust has found root in many of our hearts.

The Rev. Theodore Edson, S. T. D., the venerable Rector of St. Anne's Church, and Chaplain of the Day, then read the Litany from the Book of Common Prayer, the responses being sung by St. Anne's Choir, consisting of Mrs. Mary E. Rix, soprano, Miss Abby J. Owen, alto, William Wirt, tenor, and Frank W. S. Daly, basso, under the direction of Benjamin Walker, organist and musical director of St. Anne's Church. The Litany was supplemented by the following prayer, by the Chaplain:

O Lord, our Heavenly Father, the High and Mighty Ruler of the Universe, Who dost from Thy throne behold all the dwellers upon earth; most heartily we beseech Thee with Thy favor to behold and bless Thy servants, the President of these United States and all others in authority—the Governor of this Commonwealth and all holding office and position under him—the head of this municipality and all joined with him in the administration of the same. Let the shining of Thy countenance lighten our beloved city. May we remember gratefully Thy fatherly hand in its early and rapid growth, the direction which Thy good Providence did give to its moulding and shaping influences, through successive years developing characteristic features, bringing out and guiding popular energies to the securing of great interests and establishing important institutions. And we humbly pray that as in the past up to this marked moment of our community, so in the future, through periods of lesser or larger cycles Thy favored people may rejoice in Divine goodness; that parents and children, from generation to generation trained in the fear of God and in the blessedness of His love may be gathered into the heavenly city of His eternal and everlasting kingdom, through Jesus Christ, our Lord. Amen.

The President.—Ladies and Gentlemen, the Orator of the Day needs no introduction to a Lowell audience. It is sufficient for me merely to announce Major-General Butler.

ORATION

By Hon. B. F. Butler.

My Friends and Neighbors: On this half-centennial anniversary of the incorporation of our city as a municipality, I have been complimented by the invitation of your committee of arrangements to give you some reminiscences of the growth and early condition of our city and the men who made it what it is. The reason of this choice I assume to be that my coming here was nearer fifty years ago than that of any one else who would undertake the task.

Your attention is therefore invited neither to an oration, could I make one, nor an essay, philosophical or other.

Forty-eight years ago, less forty days, a slender boy of less than ten years with a foxskin cap closely drawn over his ears, linsey-woolsey jacket, tightly buttoned to his throat, from New Hampshire, came walking along the winding road that then led over Christian Hill, in Dracut, from Methuen, one cloudless spring afternoon, keeping pace with a country sleigh drawn by a jaded and slow-pacing horse, picking his way from snowdrift to snowdrift, which alternated with bare spots, denuded by the early rains, not driven by, but dragging an elderly man who solaced himself and steadied his nerves, set all tingling by the excruciating creaking of the steel-shod runners as they struck fire on the granite pebbles quite often, with huge pinches of yellow snuff.

As the boy reached the crest of Christian Hill, just at the right of the reservoir, the panorama of the valley at the confluence at the Concord and Merrimac rivers spread out before him, glistened in the sunlight, so that the picture is nearly as vivid now to his memory as when it first struck his wondering eyes.

If those who came here long afterwards or were born here would like to know how our present populous, well-built, flourishing city, second in importance only to the capital of the state, then looked, I will try to sketch the picture.

Far up the river to the right, glimpse was caught of a cluster of low, wooden buildings around the head of Pawtucket bridge which spanned the river over low piers showing just above the swift whirling mass of waters unseen because of the fringe of trees bordering the northern river-bank. Next stood in bold relief the building known as the "stone house," with its open verandahs next to, and commanding a beautiful view of, the falls, now enlarged and improved, the residence of our enterprising fellow-citizen, Doctor Ayer.

To the left a group of huts, part with mud walls roofed with slabs, with here and there a small white frame house. Near them stood, at a place called the "Acre" afterwards (because the subject of an almost interminable litigation) surrounding the spot where now the magnificent edifice of the first Catholic church rears its illuminated cross for the adoration of its worshippers.

With the exception of an old, weather-beaten frame house, then and now standing near the water at the foot of the falls, no building caught the eye till it met a few straggling ones surmounted by the spire of the First Congregational Church.

Nearly in line were seen three small, and what would now be deemed insignificant brick mills of the Merrimack corporation, flanked by two rows of detached two-story buildings, the boarding houses of the American portion of its operatives, while behind it ran a long row of one-story brick cottages then known as "John Bull's Row," because the homes of the block printers who had been imported from England to finish the then new and almost unknown fabric, American calico.

At the head of this row stood the house of John Dinely Prince, who had shortly before come to this country, by his skill to perfect the "Merrimack Prints," now the exemplar and pattern of all that class of manufactures in the United States, and the foundation of the prosperity of that most successful enterprise.

Further on could be discerned the house of Paul Moody, to whose business sagacity, ripe judgment and mechanical skill Lowell is more largely indebted perhaps than to any other, with a single exception, for its existence.

Still further to the left another cluster of cottages near another brick mill stood the homes of the machinists who in the Lowell Machine shop made the first cotton machinery, which has laid the foundation of the life and prosperity of our city, and in which were afterwards built the first locomotives that were made in this country.

Just beyond a little brick building with a tiny cupola, lay nestled among the forest trees near the present Northern depot, the Lowell Brewery, a prime necessity, because where there are Englishmen there must be beer.

The next line of the vista showed St. Anne's Church and parsonage, flanked on the left by a row of small ten foot wooden buildings on the south side of Merrimack Street, being the only buildings on Merrimack or Central Street, down to Middle Street, not then even marked out. Further along the same line, but a little below it, was seen a low brick house, still standing, at the junction of Middle and Central Streets.

Casting the eye a little further to the left it encountered the long snake-like-looking structure spanning the river, the then "Central Bridge," with one or two small frame houses near it on the Dracut side of the river, and beyond stood a white wooden villa, then the residence of Kirk Boott, occupying the site of the present Boot Corporation, with a large garden running back to the river, the front with a very considerable lawn before it, being very nearly opposite Central Street.

Still further to the left on a high bluff of sand occupying the point of land between the bridge and the junction of the Concord River stood another tavern, known as the "Mansion House," then I believe in charge of our respected, honored, and aged fellow citizen, who may be said to be, so far as age and ownership of the soil gives title, the only living father of Lowell, Jonathan Tyler.

As the eye passed on it took in two mills of the Hamilton Corporation with two blocks of boarding houses in front of them. Then passing the glance up Central Street came a row of small wooden buildings on the easterly side of that street, there being only a pole fence protecting a line of white birch and alder bushes on the other.

The eye struck a few wooden frame buildings clustered nearly around a small white chapel, which was the first Methodist Church, which gave its name to Chapel Hill.

Still further to the left is a small brick building, being the first considerable woolen mill in the state, occupying the site of the Middlesex Mills, and a somewhat larger wooden building, which is still in existence, at the Wamesit Power Company, where a grove of trees then hid the powder establishment of Oliver M. Whipple, the view being broken by Ira Frye's tavern, now the "American House," and by Levi Carter's tavern, now the "Washington House," and the brick building adjoining thereto.

The First Baptist Church stood out by itself in an open lot a little further to the left where the Rev. Mr. Freeman was then preaching his trial sermons prior to his installation in the following June.

Further to the left was seen the bridge across the Concord River with a few straggling buildings near it on the Belvidere side, one of which is the present brick building now standing next the bridge, and some small work-shops not to be dignified by the name of factories, where the Belvidere Manufacturing Company's buildings now stand and a few scattered frame buildings around them.

On the bluff above, where St. John's Hospital stands, towered the commanding residence of Judge Livermore, with a well kept lawn before it adorned with poplars. Then the view became lost in the magnificent woodlands that covered Reservoir Hill, and extended far down into Tewksbury where now are some of the most elegant residences of our city.

Such was the panoramic view of your infant city as it burst upon the eye of the astonished boy. By far the largest town he had ever seen, and by far the most magnificent view that had ever greeted his eyes. Nor, for beauty of sky shutting down on woodland scenery, for clustering dwellings, for rushing river and whirling waters, never since has a more noble view greeted the eye of the man after nearly fifty years.

Standing as he has lately done upon the same spot and looking upon the same sky, with land and water, covered with the population and industries of our busy city, the great change that has taken place within his memory is scarcely to be realized—a change most interesting because it is typical of the growth of our country, not more wonderful, however, than those upon our western border.

Then only a small cluster of buildings marked the city of Buffalo. A still smaller cluster around the steamboat landing was all there was of Cincinnati, and Pittsburgh was known only as a hamlet at the head waters of navigation of the Ohio, while at St. Louis, which now claims to draw to it the capitol of the nation, consisted in its most important features of its buildings built by the French and Spanish habitants of Louisiana purchased by our government of Napoleon scarcely twenty-five years before, and Chicago the extent of whose commerce and business enterprises threatens soon to rival New York, with a claim to be ranked among the first cities of the globe, had hardly a dwelling in it more important in comparison with its present palaces, than the burrow of the animal from the Indian appellation of which it is said to take its name.

After a long pause to take the scene, the boy walked on, overtook and got into the sleigh at Central Bridge to save his toll, and found shelter for the night in the brick building adjacent to Carter's tavern, spending the evening in witnessing the legerdemain tricks of one Potter, " a slight-of-hand-man," as he was then denominated, of considerable local celebrity. But there was nothing so wonderful to him in the magician-like tricks of the performer as the boy saw the next morning when he went out under a spreading oak tree standing where the buildings of " Tower's Corner " now stand and found there displayed on a bench on the open shell the first oysters that he ever saw, and was informed by the obliging standkeeper in reply to his anxious inquiry what they were for, that they were good to eat.

The boy bought one oyster and tried the experiment of swallowing it which he did not repeat for some years afterwards, satisfied by his first experiment that these strange animals were not for his eating.

All around was vacant open land stretching far away to where the Northern Depot now stands. Charles, Summer and Tyler Streets were a bog; and where the canal crosses Central Street so covered with buildings as to be entirely concealed from view, and running up to the present site of the Lowell Company's Works, and covering Market Street, was an open pond, and still further up beyond the Lowell Machine Shop, and all that region now filled with busy industry a swamp which gave the name to the locks on the canal there, " Swamp Locks " by which they were known for many years after.

If I have been successful in bringing to your minds, with your knowledge of localities, the condition of Lowell forty-eight years ago, having within its borders scarcely two thousand souls, you will mentally compare it with its present condition of more than forty thousand inhabitants, teeming with its most successful industries, being in fact the industrial capital of the state, and perhaps of the nation, speaking only of those cities where manufacturing is alone carried on as the occupation of their people.

What has wrought this change? Its origin was the sagacity and foresightedness of a few men. Its completion and fruition, the industry and thrift of our people, the integrity of our business men, and more than all the necessity for leaving here a portion, if only that of what is earned by our operatives.

With the exception of the early investment of capital in mills, and machinery, not a tenth of what they now represent, very little money has been brought to Lowell. Our city has been a hive of industry, and as a rule the honey has been gathered by others. But the early business sagacity of the managers of the large manufacturing concerns, which required that a sum should be yearly set aside from our earnings to make good all depreciation, repair and keep preserved our methods of manufacture and machinery in pace with the inventive genius of the age, has from time to time caused an extension of our works here so that in these same manufacturing establishments, the number of spindles increased from two hundred to four hundred thousand, or just double in ten years, and all without any investment of capital from abroad. Indeed, the great drawback upon the prosperity and growth of our city without which it is safe to assume that we should have doubled our present wonderful increase, has been that the owners of our mill property here, did not live here, and give our city the advantage of their expenditure, their public spirit and the investment and the rei-nvestment of the money earned by our citizens under their own eye, in the place where it was earned.

Another cause which retarded our prosperity, quite frequently overlooked, came in the years 1848-9, and was the discovery of gold in California. Those listening to me past the middle age of life who can throw their minds back to that period, will remember that was quite the darkest time Lowell has ever known, and for the reason that in addition to the fact that the dividends earned here, just alluded to, were not spent here the enterprise and spirit of our young men were drawn by the stories of fabulous wealth to be had in California. During that fever we lost nearly fifteen hundred young and middle-aged men, who left us for the golden state, and they were among the best, most energetic and most enterprising of our citizens or they would not have had the energy to go.

Assuming for safety's sake in statement that the number is overrated, and that but twelve hundred went in those years, and it would be safe to say, that, then averaging the amount of capital they took away with them, that one thousand apiece would be a low sum, and it will be seen that in addition to the loss of the labor and enterprise of these men to our growing city, and the diminution of population by the absence of their families, there was an actual withdrawal from us of some million and a quarter of capital actually here.

In spite of these several drawbacks to which I have hinted, I believe in the future Lowell can look forward with the brightest hopes of prospective increase in wealth and population in a manifold increasing ratio, that in two decades more she will double her present population.

To this view it has been objected that our water power being substantially exhausted, Lowell has nearly reached her limit of expansion, but this seems erroneous. Other cities have grown quite to rival us in some branches of our production, which were not dependent upon water power at all.

Who shall say that in the next ten years another of God's good gifts to man through inventive genius may not be received by the finding of a motive power still cheaper and more effective than steam? and in such a case where better than in Lowell can the energies of such power for manufacturing purposes be applied?

But even if steam shall continue to be the only motive power that for a generation may come in competition with water, still, by the cheapening of transportation through the net work of railways that now centre here. and still more by the use of our river for its pristine purposes of navigation, which, now improved, connects us with the sea with but a single mile of difficulties to be overcome, so that bringing here water-borne fuel, and sending away our productions by water on the cheap highway of nations, Lowell will be a point at which steam power can be had as cheap as the power furnished by the Merrimack and the Concord, pouring over the falls of their rocky beds, and our city with tenfold energy and rapidity will continue on her glorious career of prosperity, riches and doubling population.

In addition to all these, another cause of increase is most surely at work.

Our citizens are now beginning to acquire capital of their own; they are organizing industries fruitful in return to be spent and invested here, because their owners live here, and the business interests outside the great manufacturing in wool and cotton is approximating in no slow steps in value to those enterprises upon which Lowell in her earlier years solely depended.

Thus having much more largely in the future the actual results of our own earnings to invest and reinvest *here;* the actual owners of our capital realizing its results and spending its incomes *here;* turning their thoughts, wishes, hopes and inspirations toward beautifying their dwellings *here;* enriching it with grand public buildings filled with beautiful works of art and the treasures of libraries, for intellectual culture of their fellow citizens *here ;* and dying leaving to our city, and not to some far distant town or college, the rich legacies which should cultivate our children and sustain our noble charities *here*, now solely dependent on what can be spared by living workmen and women *here ;* in a word to rid ourselves of *absenteeism* by a population born here with all their memories of home nativity and pride of birth place, and desire to perpetuate a family name in kind remembrance *here ;* then shall our beloved city start anew in a most majical growth on a renewed career of prosperity that shall leave far behind our rivals, Worcester and Fall River, which have almost caught up with us because of their advantages of home capital and capitalists which I have sketched, which they have enjoyed and we have not, so that our children and their children who shall stand here where we now stand, on the next fiftieth anniversary of this day, shall with pride and joy hail this city of their nativity and of their fathers' homes, as without peer or rival in their affection and love in all that civilization may do for man, as well as in power, wealth, population, home and glory as the creation of our industry, and their fathers' and their own capital, energy, enterprise and sagacity, as we now give grateful credit to those who have gone before us, for what they have so wonderfully done under so many and so great difficulties.

It is but fitting that we should pause here and pay some tribute of remembrance to those to whom our beloved city is most indebted, although they are so many that but few within the hour allotted to me can be mentioned.

First and foremost of the remarkable men who were its founders stands the name of Kirk Boott. The owners of the mills at Waltham in 1821, were looking about for water-power by which to enlarge their means of manufacturing by their system, known as the "Waltham System," when their attention was directed by Mr. Paul Moody to the Falls of Pawtucket, the water-power of which was then utilized only by a dilapidated saw-mill. Civil engineers were sent here to make an examination, and reported that there was no water-power here on the Merrimack River. They did not seem even to have examined the Concord. What were the grounds of that opinion we have no record ; but we must remember that hydraulic engineering was then in its very infancy, and not at all understood as now.

It is one of the boasts of our city that the Merrimack River water-power, and the necessities of its successful development, has trained up by skillful pratice added to thorough theoretical education, admittedly the first hydraulic engineer in all its branches, that this country has produced, and of such sagacity, even in his younger days, as to foresee and provide for the contingency that by a sudden and not unprecedented rise of our river the obstructive works might be washed away, and the river assume its ancient bed, whose foaming waters can hardly be doubted once poured through our most thickly crowded business streets. Many years after he enjoyed a well earned triumph of his profession to see the device he had made brought into active and successful use, turning away the danger from his neighbors, and preserving the works under his charge from destruction.

I have said that the early engineers reported no water-power here, and it remained for an English half-pay cavalry officer, wandering along the side of our fall, rod in hand, casting the fly for the salmon, to discover and appreciate the mechanical force of a river which now does the work daily of ten thousand horses with only the expense of keeping them in their harness. Kirk Boott reported this view of the capabilities of the Merrimack River to Patrick T. Jackson, which view was confirmed by Paul Moody, and hence we have Lowell and this Semi-Centennial Celebration.

While to the mechanical skill of Mr. Moody and to the executive ability of Mr. Boott we are indebted for the inception of our cotton manufactures, to the business enterprise of Mr. Thomas Hurd, who did not succeed so as to realize the fruit of his labors, we are indebted for the woolen manufacture of Lowell.

Let us not forget also that to Claudius Wilson, Alexander Wright and Israel Whitney we owe the establishment of the worsted and carpet business here; the first to any considerable extent in New England or the United States, and that here was first planned and put in operation the power loom, that most wonderful emanation of human ingenuity for weaving carpet, the product of the genius of E. B. Bigelow.

But there are other evidences of the sagacity of the founders of the "Waltham System," from the effects of which Lowell yet receives an impulse, i. e,, the care taken by that system of the moral, intellectual and physical welfare of the operatives in their mills. They also provided by stringent rules that the moral and physical well-being of their operatives should be still under their charge, in a very considerable degree when not employed in labor.

The school-house and church went hand in hand with the spinning jenny. The first and in that day very large donations of the Merrimack Company and the Locks and Canals Company, the one in building and the other in aiding by denoting the site for building the two principal churches at that time in the city, St. Anne's Church and the First Congregational were the first steps in that policy.

These cautious and shrewd business men during their lives, looked upon the investment in the church as equally profitable to them as the investment in the water-power, one supplementing the other, and when those that came after them saw fit to take away from the congregation worshipping at the church what their fathers had dedicated to God, and required that money be paid back into the treasury for the purpose of dividends, which had once been expended for religious uses, there were some who predicted that the time would come when that money even would not be sufficient to eke out a dividend to the sons of the donors, and without claiming as some perhaps more devout may do, that the steady decadence from that time of those dividends until they have now stopped was in consequence of the interposition of divine wrath for the sacrilege, yet, we can well see that religious training, high morals and intelligence have made the very best working men and women in all grades of industry, and are worth many dollars in gold to those who make the most wise use of them, and the same improvidence which led to breaking up the skilled organization of some of the mills during the war, and leaving their operatives without employment, in order to sell their cotton as a speculation to supply English capital with business was but an exhibition of the same improvidence which caused the divorce of our manufacturers from any obligation to aid their operatives in supplying themselves with religious culture and teaching.

Our business had another boast. Nowhere has there been a better or more efficient system of public schools from the beginning. Each child who has desired a common school education has had it.

The schools of Lowell have been the foster nurses of men who have been and are now carrying on the greatest concerns of the country. That many of them are alive, and some in this presence is sufficient reason for no names being mentioned; but governors of states, skilled engineers, successful conductors of railroads, men energetic and successful in every department of business and human industry have gone out from our schools, and while I am obliged to advert to the fact that in the earlier discussions of the school question, some of the mill owners and notably Mr. Boot, agreed with reluctance to the early very large expenditures for schools, yet I do so in order to place credit where credit is due, and I can do this without breaking the rule that I have made to mention no names here in praise or blame of living men, because the man to whom the schools of Lowell are more indebted than any other man; who fostered them, protected them, at personal sacrifice in their infancy, who braved the opposition of those most powerful in the day when he stood up alone to speak for our schools, when the most experienced and able counsel were employed to argue against him in the Lowell town meeting; who twice over carried the vote, twelve at the first time and thirty-eight majority at the second only, by which our school system was in fact established, bears a name endeared to us all, by almost patriarchal age, by reverential feeling of esteem and love.

By universal acclaim all agree to the name of Thedore Edson.

Our city also has been peculiarly fortunate in the attainments of its medical profession, and the doctor has been honored here as nowhere else. Our first mayor was a physician, elected and re-elected as long as he would permit us so to do, and the name of Elisha Bartlett in my earlier days was a household word for all that was good, pure, learned, and intellectual in every walk of life. Subsequently our city re-elected Elisha Huntington eight times to be its mayor. I am ashamed to say it but we never elected any of our distinguished lawyers to serve as mayor so long all their terms of service put together, as we did this one physician. And yet among our lawyers there were "giants in those days." Lawrence, Mann, Williams, Locke, Hopkinson, Robinson, Wright, Brown, Wentworth, were men whose talents, learning and success would adorn the proudest bar in the United States.

It is to the credit of our citizens that while they attended to the schools they by no means neglected the needs of our young population for moral culture. Almost every sect had its church edifice where religious instruction according to its tenets was had, and it can safely be said that in no town or city of the same number of inhabitants was and is there a greater average attendance at church. And this was all the more wonderful because these church orginazations had to be carried on and churches built by a population, almost every man and woman of which were day laborers earning their daily bread, and how freely have they given up their limited substance, the many spires and church towers that can be counted from the neighboring hills iu every part of the city, most fully attest.

The result has been that no aggregate population of the same size has been more noted for its good order, quiet and honest integrity. No stupendous crimes, and comparatively but very few of the ordinary transgessions have thus far disgraced our town, so that no other city in the United States of the same number of inhabitants can show so clean a criminal record as ours, and when that record is read the very largest portion will be simple breaches of necessary police regulations.

At a very early day, the very earliest institution of the kind in the state or in the country, the "Mechanics' Association" for mutual culture and improvement, which still exists with its well stocked library, was founded here as well by the liberality of the mill owners as the contributions of those who labored.

The sick and dying have been well cared for. As early as 1837 the only residence in the city which could by any exaggeration of speech be called sumptuous or luxurious was turned into a hospital in which the sick and wounded operatives at a nominal price could receive medical and surgical treatment under the care of one of the most eminent surgeons of the United States.

It was early thought that the large influx of the foreign born which our manufacturing necessities brought together here, would be detrimental to our growth and prosperity, nay, so that the want of good order and an ill disposed element in the city would render it undesirable as a residence. But all this was a mistake. They too have built expensive and the most costly church edifices; have established schools for the teaching of their own tenets of religion, and hospitals for the care of their sick, and their children are now with us and among us and a part of us, some of the most enterprising, reliable and honored of our citizens.

There was another class of men mention of whom must be made. Attracted here in our earlier days, men came and set up business for themselves, disconnected with our mills, and brought their varied industries and interests into our city, which have been the main stay of our population in the vicissitudes of the prosperity of cotton and woolen manufacturing. Among them was a young man who came here before the incorporation of the town even, the event we celebrate.

Among the earliest, and at that time some of the very best buildings, were the fruits of his energy and enterprise. With the keenest sagacity he saw early that the future of Lowell depended upon the cheapness of transportation to tide-water, and he spent the latter part of his life in an endeavor to open such channels of communication and to save us from the effects of a single railway, which he believed to be, and feared its power as a monopoly. All his honestly acquired and hard earned wealth was invested here, and he has left behind him the only residence that may be denominated palatial, and extensive business blocks as his monument in Lowell. But he will be remembered still longer and more gratefully by us because of his efforts to secure the future prosperity of the city of his adoption by given us the benefit of cheap transportation, which I have already considered the prime necessity of our future growth. To the older citizens I need not call his name to bring him up in remembrance, and the younger have learned from their fathers to revere the memory of William Livingston, as one to whom Lowell owes very much.

Later came two brothers with their considerable wealth, acquired elsewhere, which they invested in buying up the then vacant lands east of the Concord River, in laying out streets, erecting buildings, and indeed it is not too much to say, being founders of the most beautiful part of our town, "Belvidere," which they adorned with their own residences, then the most considerable in the city, and the younger of them introduced and fostered several private manufacturing enterprises which we now so well know are so necessary to our growth. He was honored by the state with high political preferment, and the name of Nesmith will hereafter be reckoned among those who were the benefactors of Lowell.

Still another man with his great energy and skillful business combination has impressed himself upon a portion of our city.

GEN. BUTLER'S ORATION. 49

Coming here a poor boy from Vermont long before the water-power of the Merrimack had been utilized, he established a manufactory of powder at the upper falls of the Concord and carried it on for more than twenty years with great success, and with large accretion of wealth to himself, until the growing city had so encroached upon it that it was no longer safe; and then by a canal constructed with his own private means he so utilized the water-power of the Concord River at that point as to develop six hundred more horse power to be used in varied manufactures which even in his time had brought to that part of the city and connected therewith a larger population and more wealth than the whole limits of the city contained at the time of its incorporation as a town. Enjoying largely the confidence of his fellow-citizens, many times elected to offices in guidance of its affairs, while his memory may have passed from the younger portion of our citizens yet hereafter there will be found inscribed on the roll of the founders of Lowell in no subordinate place the name of Oliver M. Whipple.

The busy hands of the clock warn me that I must pass over the many other honored names of esteemed citizens now passed away, who deserve honorable mention at this hour and our most grateful remembrance. Tradition, ripening into history, will do justice to their memories, and the future historian of Lowell will give them the place they most fully deserve.

There is still another topic which justice to the gallant and noble dead will not allow me to pass in silence; whose deeds throw the most brilliant lustre upon the bright escutcheon of the fame of our city. While other towns and cities in the County of Middlesex claim the high honor of the first blood shed in the war of the Revolution to obtain our liberty, Lowell, the younger sister of them all, has the still greater glory of the first blood shed in the streets of Baltimore in the war for preservation of those liberties and the free government which owes its birth to Lexington and Concord. Our city can point with justifiable pride to the fact that a regiment of her soldiers were first welcomed at the nation's capital as its saviour, and was the first and only, and I trust will be the last regiment, who found their bivouac in the Senate chamber of the United States.

Fired by the patriotic examples of these, her patriots, who, as minute men, first answered to the call to arms to save the nation's life, Lowell poured forth her sons without stint or measure to the armies of the Union, so that no considerable battle was fought east of the Alleghanies where the blood of a Lowell soldier was not shed, and no collection of graves of those who died for their country by disease more deadly than the bullet, is complete unless it contains the mouldering ashes of some son of Lowell, his blood yielded up in behalf of his country's life. I need not here call the roll of these our sons and brothers, so glorious, not only in our city's own history, but in the history of our country.

Sorrowing hearts of weeping wives, mothers, daughters, sisters, brothers, sons, and fathers have not yet ceased to bleed for the loss of their dear ones, who are now remembered in anguish, but whose memories will, when the soft touch of the magic hand of time has soothed all grief, shine forth with vivid recollection of their valor, their patriotism and their sacrifices. There is no need of giving their history here. Go read the history of your country in the day of its most perilous hour, and there their names are inscribed and enshrined forever.

Now my task is ended,—imperfectly done I feel in every part. Yet if it has aided to bring to the mind of the young of this assembly the names of those whom they and their children should delight to honor so that their virtues and example may be transmitted from father to son until a future day when those of us who now remember them, and were some of us their compeers, have passed from earth, on the centennial birth of our town their names may be kept in bright remembrance, I shall have accomplished all and more than I hoped.

More than all besides, let us not forget that those who have gone before us have committed as a sacred trust this our beloved city to our care, its prosperity to our foresight, energy and integrity. Let us see to it that secular and religious teaching shall find the same high place and fostering care with us that our predecessors gave to both ; that integrity of life, order in business, openhanded and liberal charity, public spirit and patriotism shall be ours as it was theirs ; that we may transmit to the next generation, improved, enriched, beautified and adorned, a city more prosperous, of more honor to the state and country than we received from them, so that he who shall stand in my place fifty years hence may have cause to note how we have done our duty to our fellow men in the several walks of life to which we are called, as I have feebly attempted to do in recalling the memories of some of those who have gone before.

The President.—Mr. Appleton, in his history, says that one day, in Boston, he chanced to meet Mr. Boott, and he said to him : "The

GEN. BUTLER'S ORATION. 51

Legislature is about to pass a bill for the incorporation of our part of Chelmsford, and there is only one thing necessary,—that is, the adoption of a name; and there seem to be two names in question,—Lowell and Derby." "By all means," said Mr. Appleton, "call it Lowell." Ladies and gentlemen, we have here to-day a relative of him for whom our city is named,—a son-in-law and nephew of Mr. Francis Cabot Lowell,—John A. Lowell, of Boston, who will now address you. [Loud applause.]

ADDRESS

By Hon. John A. Lowell.

I thank you sincerely, ladies and gentlemen, for this cordial welcome, although I am very well aware that it is not because of anything I have done in connection with this city, although I was at the head of the Boott and Massachusetts Mills, both of which I built. I am aware, also, that it is not for the reason that Mr. John Lowell, Jr., who was the founder of the Lowell Institute, resided for some years in this town,—first in a stone house on the Merrimack River, and subsequently in Belvidere. I am further aware that it is not owing to the fact that the second treasurer of the Merrimack Mills, the one who succeeded Mr. Boott, Francis Cabot Lowell, was the son and bore the name of the person for whom the town was named. I am aware that I am indebted for this reception to the interest which some of you may feel in the merits and the life of him for whom this city was named.

Of all the persons who were interested at that time in the building up of this new town of Lowell, I am perhaps the only survivor; at least, the only one with such health as to enable him to participate in these proceedings. And although this is the first time I was ever on a public platform,—and I hope it will be the last,—I feel that it is incumbent on me to at least do as much as to give you some personal reminiscences,—reminiscences which very often get considerably altered as time advances, and the original actors in the events described are removed by death.

For several years prior to 1812, we had enjoyed in this country almost a monopoly of the carrying trade of Europe. We had enjoyed it because, owing to the war which existed between Napoleon Bonaparte and England, all the ports in Europe had been closed to Great Britain. The continental States did not permit the introduction of

English goods, and as England did not like to have any other goods entered, she had declared all the seaboard countries of Europe to be under blockade. As the quarrel proceeded, the English found that the Americans were doing what they thought belonged to them; that they were carrying spices, sugar, coffee, and everything else from the East and West Indies to those ports in Europe; and in order to counteract that, the English devised this system, that every vessel that was going to any port in Europe from this country should first touch at a British port, and there take out a license. Those were the famous "Orders in Council" which were passed by England. Napoleon did not like this action on the part of England, and therefore passed certain decrees which were well known at that time as the Berlin and Milan decrees. Those decrees were, that any vessel that entered any port of Europe armed with a British license should have her cargo confiscated. American commerce was thus placed in a very embarrassing position. If our merchants attempted to avoid Scylla, they fell into Charybdis. If they took an English license, their cargoes were confiscated; if they did not take it, the British would not allow them to enter any European port. That was the state in which our commerce was at that time. In New England, it was even worse than that, for trade was going very rapidly away to New York, because, there being no railroads at that time, the Hudson River, gave great advantages to New York. But a young Bostonian, whom nature had designed for a statesman, but fortune had made a merchant, was at that time in Edinburgh, and he pondered over these things. What was to become of this country, especially if the war should last twenty years? It was thought at that time that war would be declared between this country and England, and war was declared, in 1812. Napoleon at that time appeared to be in the zenith of his power. Our Government at Washington never dreamed that two years would upset him completely; therefore they did the wisest thing they could; they declared war against England. This young man of whom I speak pondered these things deeply. It was Francis Cabot Lowell, a young man at that time thirty-five years of age, whose business had been that of a merchant, but who had been driven from his business, at first by the embargo, afterwards by the non-intercourse act, and finally, by war. In thinking over what could be done to employ the industry of this country, he naturally turned his thoughts to the cotton manufacture, which at that time, had been greatly developed in England, and had created some princely fortunes. In fact, it had furnished the backbone of the war. Without it, England would not have been able to carry on, almost single-handed, the struggle wi h Napoleon. He thought it was possible that that could be introduced into the United States. Certainly it could be done, if the war was to last thirty years, as the war in Germany had lasted, or even twenty-five like the wars of the Revolution. But he was cautious as well, and he said, " Suppose the war does not last; suppose it only lasts the time necessary to build a factory and put it in operation, and then peace comes,"—and that turned out to be the fact,—" then what will happen?" Thinking over that matter, he said to himself,—"The English have great advantages; they have an unlimited amount of capital; they have very cheap labor. How can we compete with them? In the first place, we can have joint-stock companies, and by combining the capital of men of smaller means togeth we can make it equivalent to the capital of one man who is very much richer. Then the ingenuity of my countrymen will enable them to invent machinery, which will go far to supersede the necessity of having so much labor. Then the raw material can be got much more cheaply than in Europe, especially if the war continues." He therefore determined that the thing could be done, and he said it should be done. That was the nature of the man. He immediately went to work to examine, as far as he was permitted to do, all the establishments then existing in England. He went to Manchester and other places, and examined carefully their works. There were certain things to which he could not obtain access. One was the power loom, which had been invented by Cartwright sometime before, and which was a monopoly; no plans of it had been published, and he could not get any description of it. He determined, however, that the thing could be done. He came out to this country in a cartel, during the war, and the first thing he did after arriving here was to take into his counsels his brother-in-law, Patrick Tracy Jackson, who, like himself, had been driven from commerce, having been a supercargo for a long while, by the war. His next step was to engage the services of Paul Moody, of Amesbury, who was then well known as a skilful mechanician. He then went in search of a water-power, and found one that suited him at Bemis's Paper Mill, in Waltham, and bought that. It was not until he had done all these things that he put himself into communication with Mr. Nathan Appleton. He offered Mr. Appleton stock to the amount of ten thousand dollars in this new enterprise. Mr. Appleton said he could not afford to invest so much as that in so hazardous an enterprise, but he would take five thousand dollars, which he did. The power loom, as I said before, they had no drawings of, and could not get at all. It was necessary, therefore, to re-invent it. It was necessary, in fact, to re-invent a great deal of the machinery, because they conceived the bold idea of carrying on every process, from the first coming in of the cotton to the going out of the finished cloth, in one mill,—a thing which had never been done before. It was therefore necessary that all the machinery should be adapted to that purpose.

Mr. Appleton, in his account of the introduction of the power-loom, states that Mr. Lowell, though no mechanic, no mechanician, invented that himself. He shut himself up in an upper room in Broad Street, hired a man to turn a crank, and there made experiments, day after day, week after week, until they were crowned with perfect success. In the meantime, Mr. Paul Moody had been at work upon the rest of the machinery : the throstle-spindle, which it was thought necessary to have at that time, on account of the heavy goods it was proposed to make,—the heavy cottons of India; the double-speeder; the drawing-frame,—all these machines were re-invented by Mr. Moody. In inventing the double-speeder, which was quite a different machine from the English fly-frame, he was obliged to introduce some motion which required accurate mathematical calculations. The double-cone in that instrument effecting the winding on spools directly, without the intervention of any other machine, it became necessary that it should be an exactly calculated motion. The calculations for this motion were made by Mr. Lowell entirely, and years after, when there was a suit in regard to the patent right of the double-speeder, Dr. Bowditch, being called in as a witness said he had studied those calculations with admiration, as they contained some simplifications which he had not known before that anybody possessed in the United States Such was the character of Mr. Lowell.

When he came to put his mill in operation at Waltham, there was, of course, great rejoicing. When the first pieces of goods were turned out, so small was the belief in the possibility of such a thing, that they could not be sold in Boston. The dealers said, "No, it can't be possible. There is some mistake about it, and we won't buy the goods." A few of the goods were put up at auction, and they brought something over thirty cents a yard,—which of course was a great triumph at that time.

Mr. Lowell, in addition to that, went into Rhode Island, to see what there was there, and what rivalry might be expected from that quarter. He found that almost every spindle in Rhode Island was stopped. Peace had then taken place, and the introduction of English goods was such that every spindle, except a few in Slater's Mill, was stopped. For at that time, there was no such thing as a mill, as we understand it now. They were all merely spinning mills. The probability is (Mr. Appleton gives that as his opinion, and I have no doubt it was so), that the first mill built in Waltham, with 1790 spindles, was the only mill, not simply in the United States, but in the world, where the cotton was taken in at one end, and turned out finished cloth at the other. The whole of that idea was Mr. Lowell's.

Then Mr. Lowell had another idea in his mind, which was one of the greatest importance, and that was the moral and religious instruction of the operatives. He was going to introduce this business for American girls (at that time, we were not overrun with Irish); he therefore wished, and thought it necessary, in order to attract that class of population, in order to enable parents to feel safe in leaving their children at these mills, to institute an entirely new system, different from the English. In England, and on the continent of Europe, the operatives in the mills were sordid, vicious, and every way degraded. He determined that it should not be so here, and therefore built boarding-houses for the operatives, put them under the care of matrons selected for that purpose, allowing no man to sleep under the same roof with them. He also instituted schools that should be free for the children of the operatives; paid their pew taxes, allowing them to go to whatever churches they chose. All that system, which has been so much admired by every foreigner who has visited this country was introduced by Mr. Lowell, and Mr. Lowell alone. To that Mr. Nathan Appleton bears testimony in his book. He says that Mr. Jackson and Mr. Moody were men of unrivalled talent, and of great energy, but that Mr. Lowell was the informing soul of the whole proceeding. I think that cannot be denied.

It was only this morning that I received a book containing the papers that were read before the Old Residents' Association of this city or town, wh ch contains very nearly the same things which I have been telling you. There was, however, one thing said there in the memoir of Kirk Boott, which I wish to have an opportunity of setting you right upon. I refer to the statement, that he, Kirk Boott, was the first person who devised the plan of a joint stock company. On that subject, the words used are these: "The carrying on of manufactures on a large scale by a joint stock company was an experiment that had not then been tested." The difficulty about that is, that in the very same volume, and but a few pages before, but by a different hand, there is an account of Mr. Lowell's first introduction of the cotton manufacture at Waltham, the whole of Waltham being made a manufacturing town, which overflowed in this direction. They came over here to try to find a place where they could extend it. In the article on Mr. Boott the whole of this is completely ignored, and the credit is given to Mr. Boott as having been the first to introduce into this country the idea of joint stock companies, as applied to cotton mills. I saw that statement only just as I was about taking the cars to come up here. I find, however, a sentence a few pages further on in the volume, which I thought might well be quoted here, only substituting the name of Mr. Lowell for that of Mr. Kirk Boott : " When the thing was to be done over again, and an entire manufacturing city was to be built, fifteen miles north, they had only to improve on his idea. The difference is like that between the original invention and subsequent improvement. He had no copy to improve upon. He had to think every thing out anew ." I think you will agree with me, that after the cotton manufacture had been established at Waltham so successfully that they were obliged to move here, not having water-power enough there, it can hardly be just to give to another person the credit of all those inventions that belong to nobody but Francis C. Lowell. I should be the last person to say one word in depreciation of Kirk Boott. He was my bosomfriend, and I was his trustee. I would not say anything to detract from his credit ; but it is no more true, as a matter of fact, that he made the first experiment in joint stock companies in carrying on the cotton manufacture, than it is true that he went out with a fishing line and found there was a water-power at Chelmsford. I pretend to know all about that thing. The first person who suggested this place was Ezra Worthen. Paul Moody knew nothing about it. Mr. Moody and Mr. Jackson came up afterwards and saw this place. It is not true that Mr. Boott was the first to suggest it. So far from it, the whole purchase was made of the Pawtucket Canal and of most of the farms here before Mr. Kirk Boott had set foot on the spot. Consequently, it could not have been Mr. Boott who found out the water-power. I do not believe that, even in those days of ignorance, any New England boy could come to a place where there was a river with a thirty-foot fall, and think there was no water-power here.

Ladies and gentlemen, there are a great many advantages in not writing a speech,—and I have not written a word. One advantage is, that you can stop when you please, another that you are not likely to fall into the error of saying, with the orator of the day, "I am warned by the hand on the clock that it is time for me to stop," and that for the simple reason that there is no clock in sight.*

---

* In a later revision of the foregoing remarks, the following paragraph was added by the speaker :—" Francis Cabot Lowell passed the winter of 1816 in Washington, and

ADDRESS

By Rt. Rev. Thomas M. Clark, D. D.

Ladies and Gentlemen : I have prepared no address for this occasion, for I knew the distinguished orator of the day well enough to feel very certain that anything I might write before hand would be anticipated by him, and I am very glad now that I committed nothing to paper.

I look upon the present as a sort of family gathering, and on this ground, perhaps, you will excuse me if, in the few remarks I have to make, I am somewhat egotistical, and refer to personal matters, which might seem somewhat out of taste on a different occasion.

One of the early recollections of my boyhood takes me back to a certain year when my respected father every little while was missing from his home in Newburyport, and went off on horseback to Chelmsford, and it was reported that he was passing the season in this region, occupying himself in hunting and fishing. I believe there was occasionally a poor wretch of a squirrel or rabbit shot and eaten up at 'Squire Whiting's, at the Falls, but most of the game that was consumed on those occasions was bought of other people. The real purpose which he had in hand was the purchase of the land on which this city now stands. That was the business in which he was engaged, not the shooting of rabbits. Now let me tell you how it happened that he was employed in this work. The firm that contracted to build the original canal, which, as you all know, was made, not for any purpose of manufacture, but simply to improve the navigation of the Merrimack, failed. My father was a clerk in the employ of that firm, and being familiar with the work, he was engaged to carry it on, and in the process of this branch of business, he became familiar with this whole region; so these gentlemen in Boston, of whom you have heard, requested him to buy the land in his own name, in order that there might be no sus-

---

procured for the protective duty of 6 1-4 cents per square yard, the support of Mr. Lowndes and Mr. Calhoun. For all these services Mr. Lowell asked no compensation. His work was now accomplished. He died the following year, at the early age of forty-two. And now, ladies and gentlemen, when we consider that, alone in his solitary closet, he worked out these splendid results, and by his energy carried them forward to perfection, in spite of the incredulity of some and the rivalry of others, that he did this with a frame already wasted by disease,—was it not a meet tribute to his memory that this city, the fruit and outcoming of his vision, that this Queen of manufacturing industry, should bear the name of LOWELL ?"

picion of the purpose to which it was to be appropriated; for if it had been foreseen that such a city as this was to stand here, the good old farmers who ploughed the soil would never have sold their land at any reasonable rate, unless human nature was very different then from what it is now. There was a great deal of speculation, I have heard him say, as to the purpose that he had in view in making this purchase of land. There was a very general impression that he intended to set up an enormous tannery here. There was one farmer who believed that he was insane, and therefore he was unwillling to take the trouble to make the deeds, transferring his farm, until 'Squire Wright signed a bond of indemnity, to the amount of two hundred dollars, guaranteeing him this sum in case it should turn out that he had taken the trouble for nothing. He was firmly satisfied that my father would never pay such prices for this land, if he was not insane. But so it went on until the whole matter was completed, when he transferred the property to the gentlemen in Boston who had employed him to make the purchase.

I have one further reminiscence, of which you will allow me to speak, in connection with this subject, and I will then pass on to something else. Six or eight years after this city was established, I was teaching school here at seven hundred dollars a year. (I think it was more than I fairly earned). At that time, my father came to the city, and said there was great consternation among the gentlemen who had established this place, for it had just then been discovered, for the first time, that although they had employed the best legal counsel, and had guarded every minor point with great sagacity, they had entirely forgotten to have my mother sign away her right of dower; so that, if my father had died at that time, she would have had a claim upon one-third of the real estate of this city; and as the real estate carried the buildings, every structure erected would have been affected by this fact. I thought it a little strange that I should be earning seven hundred dollars a year under those circumstances. I feel honored in saying that the deeds were signed as soon as they were made ready, and that no compensation was either asked or offered. Perhaps in these times, there would be a little more care exercised in such a matter, and some slight matter of fifty or a hundred thousand dollars might be asked as a compensation for the release; but in those days, we acted upon somewhat higher principles of honor than prevail to-day.

So much for that. I am sure you will pardon me for having alluded to such personal matters, because there is probably no one else living that could present some of the facts which I have just now narrated.

In the year 1831, I came to this city, and presented myself at the door of my venerable friend, the Rector of St. Anne's Church, as a candidate for the first High School ever established in Massacuusetts, outside of Boston, and perhaps in New England, and through his influence, I received the appointment. I entered upon my duties, in a little wooden building on the Hamilton Corporation, a building that might have cost, I should think, three or four hundred dollars to erect. I remember as if it were but yesterday, the snowy November morning when I wended my way to that little school-house, to enter upon the work assigned me. Forty boys and girls, a six-plate stove and a small desk crowded the building; and there I worked for a year. I remember, as occupying seats in that humble school-house, certain boys whose names have since become somewhat famous. On one bench sat the orator of the day, and whatever trouble he may have given other people, he never gave me the slightest. Perhaps it was owing to the fact that I knew Benjamin F. Butler was a boy who might be led, but could not be driven, and I conducted myself accordingly. On another bench sat Gov. Straw, of New Hampshire, now present. On another bench sat Gustavus V. Fox, of whom you have all heard, and whose noble record during our late war has made him memorable. There were others whose names I might mention, who made themselves distinguished in various ways; some who promised high things, but the rude hand of Death swept them off before the flower had had time to ripen into fruit. Their memory is blessed.

And now I desire, on this occasion, to thank my venerable father for the care and attention that he always showed to those who were in the employ of the city as teachers. You are indebted to him more than to any man for the educational institutions of this city, in its early days. He had some peculiarities. He was wonderfully kind and patient with us when we did some very foolish and improper things; and he had a way of visiting the schools, not always on set and formal occasions. We did not know exactly when he was coming, so that we were not always ready for him. That was a great advantage. It was a very proper thing to do. I think if inspectors and committees of various sorts would look in upon schools and other public institutions when they are not expected, they might see some things which they never expect to see.

But I am rambling on perhaps at too great length. I intended to say a few things, in a general way, about certain peculiarities of Lowell. In the first place, when Lowell sprang into being, it was at a leap. There had never been such a leap in the whole history of the towns and cities of the United States. When this city thus sprang into being, it was unprecedented. Chicago has made great leaps, and made great boasts of it, since. San Francisco has made great leaps; but Lowell made the first leap, and it was a marvel all over the land, that a city should have grown up here almost in a night,—a city so grand as Lowell was, even in its earlier days. Then, was it ever heard of before, that a manufacturing corporation built a church and a rectory at its own expense, and for a series of years gave the use of both free? I know that in Rhode Island there are cases where churches are in great measure sustained by the gentlemen who own the property, but I never heard of an instance precisely anologous to the present. Then, again, the intense interest manifested in public education, to which reference has already been made, was a point upon which I had intended to dwell, but it is not necessary now. Lowell stands pre-eminent for enterprise, for intelligence, and for high morals; and it is the church and the school that have done it. Do any of you remember that marvellous procession of parasols that filed through your streets when Gen. Jackson visited Lowell in 1833? There never was such a procession before; there never will be again. And what did that procession of parasols indicate? It indicated this fact: that women and girls, might be engaged as operatives in mills, and yet carry themselves like ladies; dress and appear like ladies; have all the high tone which belongs to ladies, and perhaps know more than some ladies know, and these educated women were earning their bread by the labor of their hands in the factories.

But I will not go on. It is getting late, and there are others to follow. Lowell is a typical place. It is typical of intelligence, morals, and sound religion. The world is to be set forward, not only by moral, but by material influences. The world is to be set forward, in a certain degree, and in a certain way, by machinery, which increases the amount of production, and in great measure supersedes the need of human toil; so that all this thunder of revolving wheels, and this whirl of spindles, and this rattle of looms, and this clang of ponderous hammers, sound in my ear like the Inauguration March of a new and grander epoch.

The President.—We have with us on this occasion a gentleman well known from his connection with the agricultural and horticultural societies of our country, but he comes here to-day as the President of the New England Historic-Genealogical Society, and he is the especial guest of the city on this occasion. I have now the pleasure of introducing to you the Hon. Marshall P. Wilder, of Boston.

ADDRESS

By Hon. Marshall P. Wilder.

Mr. Mayor: I thank you for the very kind manner in which you have introduced me to this audience. It is true that I am here as one of the representatives of the New England Historic-Genealogical Society, whose duty and especial province it is to treasure up, record and preserve everything that appertains to the history of our own beloved New England, to whose welfare Lowell has contributed so largely. But after the eloquent historical discourse by Gen. Butler, and the interesting address by Bishop Clark on the moral influences of this city, there is not a word left to be said by me in either direction. I rejoice most heartily in the growth and prosperity of the city of Lowell, the forerunner and pioneer, as you have heard to-day, not only in the great industrial pursuit to which New England is so much indebted, but also in those moral influences by which it has sought to elevate the girls and women who are employed here, instead of depressing them, as is too often the case in other countries. I coincide heartily with the remarks of Bishop Clark on that subject.

It was not my good fortune to be born in Lowell, but I am proud to say, that my birth was only a few miles north, on the border of New Hampshire, and from early life I have kept the run of the history of Chelmsford and Lowell; and I am happy to be here and to add a few words on this occasion. I was honored, very early in my mercantile life in Boston, with the custom of the merchants of Lowell. In fact, I can trace back my knowledge of Lowell by the courtesies which have been extended to me on many occasions, and (pardon me for saying) the many good dinners that I have partaken of here. A remark of Gen. Butler brings to my mind the fact, that one of the best dinners of which I ever partook in Lowell was from a fresh salmon, at the Coburn House, fifty years ago last June, taken from the waters of the Merrimack only about an hour before we sat down to the table.

One of the great pleasures that I experience to-day is in meeting your honored Mayor, whom I have known from a small boy, and when

I came into the hall this forenoon, and saw him addressing that assembly, it brought to my mind the blessed influences of New England education. I believe he was a good boy and hence he has become a good man. I have been for nearly forty years connected and interested with his respected father in manufactures, who, I bless God, has lived to this time, to educate and train up his child in the way he should go; and my heart rises in gratitude to the Giver of all good for the blessings of education, as illustrated in the gentleman who stands before you to-day as example of the beneficent influences of your Lowell schools.

But I must not take up your time. I was very glad to hear the orator of the day remind you of the illustrious benefactors who had founded our manufacturing cities in New England, to whom we all owe, and the whole country owes, a debt of gratitude, and I trust their names will ever be remembered among the benefactors of mankind. We reflect on what American manufactures have done for New England, we may well take pride in what has been accomplished, and look forward to the day when we may be as independent in the products of our soil, as we are in the policy of our government. I trust that Lowell, may go on, prospering and to prosper, in the future as in the past, and be an honor to itself, to the state, and to the country, and a blessing to mankind.

The President.—On the sixth day of March, 1826, the inhabitants of the town of Lowell met in their first town meeting at the Coburn Tavern. At that meeting, two gentlemen present with us to-day were elected upon the first School Committee of Lowell. I knew, as a scholar, having attended the various schools of Lowell, that one of them was always somewhat of a "terror to evil doers" in school, for when Dr. Green was sub-committee of the school, if the master said, "I am going to send you to Dr. Green," it struck a chill over that boy, that made him good for the whole term. I have the pleasure of introducing to you, ladies and gentlemen, Dr. Green, one of the first school-committee-men of Lowell, who will relate to you some historical reminiscences of our city.

HISTORICAL REMINISCENCES.

By Dr. John O. Green.

Mr. President: Seven years ago a few gentlemen came together in this city to consider the expediency of forming an Association of Old Residents to repair old friendships and to collect and treasure up the facts and incidents of our local history, so transient yet so interesting, so surely and so rapidly being crowded out of sight. The idea met with unexpected and gratifying success. A membership of over two hundred, with quarterly meetings and full attendance, and papers of value and importance, attest the success of the scheme. The action was not premature, for while we have abundant reason for congratulation in its progress and prosperity and the general favor it has met in the community, at nearly every meeting our condolence and sympathy are awakened by the deaths of those who, having shared with us the active duties and responsibilities of our citizenship, do now rest from their labors. A few, very few, who began the half-century with us here, are living and present to-day. As we date back to the very inception of our city, and have been witnesses, and actors, in the grand and novel experiment in the history of American manufactures, here and then begun, which now we see so triumphantly achieved, can you wonder that we meet you to-day and on this occasion with a sympathy which is not in the power of my poor words to describe? I should much have preferred to continue to act the part of a grateful listener, did not a sense of duty compel me to say a few words of congratulation, of retrospection and of warning.

How little should we have as an impulse to good deeds, or for our guidance in life, were it not for the history and traditions which have come down to us from former ages, the examples of the great and good, of right and wrong, as expressed in the history of nations and the lives of men!

We speak of Lowell fifty years ago as an experiment. It was indeed the first of so many similar enterprises, since undertaken, that we are apt to underrate its boldness and novelty; yet undertaken by such men, with so much forethought and cautious investigation as were sure harbingers of success.

In 1820 to the minds of Lowell and Jackson and Moody and Appleton and Boott, its elements had been so elaborated and its problems so demonstrated as to leave little room for hesitation and none for doubt. Their portraits, in yonder hall, commemorate them as the founders of the city, and, as in duty bound this day, we recognize the city itself as their enduring monument. They were sanguine of success; but we only, of to-day, can realize the limit it has reached beyond their wildest dreams.

They seek a place to begin, and Worthen chalks out upon the counting room floor, in Boston, to their admiring eyes, Pawtucket Falls and the immense and as was then supposed, the inexhaustible waterpower of the entire Merrimack. Five of them make a cautious visit to the spot.

In 1821, I quote from an eloquent sermon by Bishop Clark: "I remember in my boyhood, my father*, arriving at our home in Newburyport, and telling us that at last he had been able to effect the purchase of certain farms in old Chelmsford which he had been requested by a few gentlemen in Boston to buy in his own name and then transfer to them. The reason which led to his employment, in this service, carries us back to the latter part of the last century. The firm, in which he, as a young man, held the office of clerk, had contracted to build the old canal around the Falls of the Merrimack, with a view to the improvement of navigation; but soon after entering upon this work, a very formidable operation in those days, they failed in the business and he was thereupon employed as an agent to superintend the completion of this design. The familiarity which this labor gave him, both with the general features of the region and with individuals resident there, led to the subsequent engagement to which I have alluded. The place where your splendid city now stands, was then a swampy and not over productive piece of land and various were the speculations as to his purpose in purchasing so large a quantity of such an undesirable territory; the final conclusions being that he intended to establish an enormous tan yard which would probably be his ruin. It was considered so problematical whether he would eventually be able to pay the extravagant price which he offered for a certain portion of the land that the owner demanded a bond of indemnity to be signed by a distinguished lawyer in the vicinity, amounting to the sum of two hundred dollars, in case the deed of sale should be returned upon his hands; the good man intimating to his friends his strong persuasion that the purchaser was probably insane."

In 1822, in April, Kirk Boott arrives and the great work begins, with an energy and determination which were in strong contrast to the quiet habits of an old New England town like Old Chelmsford.

* Thomas M. Clark, Esq.

Never was a man better adapted for the position in which he was placed, by natural ability, by early education, by decision of character, by the most perfect devotion and unselfish consecration to the grand enterprise before him. He was thirty-two years of age. He spoke in an undertone, always in few words, directly to the point. Either naturally, or acquired by his military education, he had a commanding manner which never, to me, seemed misplaced, but appropriate to the position of superintendent of a vast multiplicity of affairs and a large number of men. His orders were given with briefness and precision and he expected the same in reply. When you reflect on the character of the old settlers here at the time, you will not wonder that these characteristics were often misunderstood by them, that his directness was mistaken for haughtiness and his energy for overbearing. His situation was novel. No similar enterprise had been undertaken. To be sure he had able assistants selected for the different parts of it, yet he it was, who, in all doubts, was called upon to advise and decide. The interests of the Merrimack Company, the only company at that time, and those of individual land owners, the greedy speculators in real estate, the large contractors and the selection of suitable overseers of work were seldom identical or easily reconciled. His prompt and curt replies did not always at first command a cheerful acquiescence. Yet under strong provocations he was always dignified and gentlemanly. His knowledge of men seemed almost like intuition. Under its promptings were collected here a noble band of mechanics. Men not only skilled craftsmen but men of incorruptible integrity whose lives were passed here and whose faithful works are all around us. The variety of his employments and the versatility of his talents almost exceed belief. He was engineer, architect, draughtsman, conveyancer, clerk, moderator of town meeting, usually by a unanimous vote; representative to the legislature, receiving one hundred and one votes out of one hundred and six, and a review of all his work in these departments would only go to show a remarkable correctness of judgment and wise forethought. Enthusiastic in the great problem to whose solution his whole soul was devoted, his labors scarcely knew any diminution, even after they were interrupted by his failing health, and were ended by his death in 1837, at the early age of forty-six years and four months.

In 1823 in September, the great wheel on the Merrimack corporation began to revolve; in November the first cloth was returned and the hum of machinery commenced only to be intensified and multiplied in ceaseless motion from that day to this, for more than fifty years. And here a single fact speaks volumes to the honor of all the leaders and agents of these magnificent corporations. They are, it is said, soulless, but from that day to this, in peace and war, amidst the distractions of trade, the misfortunes of commerce, individual losses and corporate bankruptcy in other places, here the monthly payments to every individual person in their employ have never been dishonored or postponed for a single day.

It was in the autumn of this year eleven acres were carefully prepared and planted with acorns to supply the demand for white oak timber in coming years.

In 1824, before the first mill had been three months in operation, the directors had decided to provide for public worship for the people in their employ, and as soon as a suitable place could be prepared for them to assemble the Rev. Rector of St. Anne's was appointed to the position he has so long and so honorably filled. "In his presence," said Bishop Clark in 1865, " we cannot say all we would of his patient, laborious, faithful ministry amongst you. The sun has not been more regular in his rising and setting than he has been in his daily round of duties.

"'At his approach complaint grew mild;
And when his hand unbarred the shutter,
The clammy lips of fever smiled
The welcome which they could not utter.'"

No storm has ever raged which he would not cheerfully face when the call of the sufferer summoned him from his fireside; no Sunday has ever dawned when the doors of St. Anne's have not been opened to the worshipper; no heavy-laden sinner ever asked his counsel and was sent uncomforted away.

"It was in this year," says Mr. Bachelder, "I well remember the prediction of Mr. Patrick Jackson. He remarked that their purchase of real estate at the Falls comprised about as many acres as were contained in the original territory of Boston before it was extended by encroachments on the tide waters; and," he continued, "if our plans succeed as we have reason to expect, we shall have as large a population on our territory in twenty years as we had in Boston twenty years ago."

This language from a sane, calculating business man appeared too extravagant for belief, but his expectations were more than realized. In 1804 the population of Boston was 26,000. In 1844 the population of Lowell must have been 28,000. By the state census in 1845 it was 28,841.

In 1825, attracted by the fame of the new town, the editor of the Essex Gazette makes a journey from Salem and August 12 in his paper thus portrays his astonishment : " As we ascended the high grounds which lie on the side of the Merrimack, the beautiful valley which has been chosen for the site of the manufacturing establishment opened upon our view. It is indeed a fairy scene. Here we beheld an extensive city, busy, noisy and thriving, with immense prospects of increasing extent and boundless wealth. Everything is fresh and green with the vigor of youth, yet perfect in all the strength of manhood. It reminds us of a Russian spring which starts, as it were, from the silence and desolation of winter into all the luxuriance and life and motion of summer. It seems as if the imagination was transported into the regions of antiquity among the Asiatic monarchs, who commanded cities to rise up and be built in a day. What cannot a combination of genius, wealth and industry produce! At the distance of about two miles above the factories are Pawtucket Falls, or rather rapids. Here the river precipitates itself over an immense bed of solid rocks which extend, from side to side, for the distance of a mile. The whole river is white with foam. No boat can pass these rapids, and this very circumstance which, for ages, has been considered an irremediable misfortune has been made a source of wonderful improvement and a benefit to the whole country. A canal commencing above the falls and winding in a semi-circular course for about two miles terminates by two locks at Concord River. A short cut from the centre of this canal into the Merrimack furnishes an *infinite* water-power, and this simple contrivance is the whole of the wonder-working power which has created a flourishing town in as short a time as is required in some places to build a log-house. On the banks of the Merrimack are already three superb factories and two immense piles of brick buildings for calico printing. In front of these, on the banks of the factory canal which is fenced in and ornamented with a row of elms, are situated the houses for the people. They are handsomely and uniformly painted and are beautifully ornamented with flower gardens in front and separated by wide avenues. There is a beautiful Gothic stone church opposite the dwelling houses and a parsonage of stone is erecting. There is a post office, fine taverns, one of which is a superb stone edifice with out-buildings of the same material, and perhaps two hundred houses all fresh from the hands of the workmen. The ground is intersected with fine roads and good bridges, The whole seems like the work of enchantment.

" About three hundred persons, two thirds of whom are females, young women from the neighboring towns, are employed. The women earn from a dollar to two dollars a week according to skill. We stood gazing at this fairy vision at the distance of a mile. The roar of the water falls is intermingled with the hum and buz of the machinery. Sometimes it would raise its voice above the roar of the waters and then die away and be lost and mingled with them in harmony. It seemed to be a song of triumph and exultation at the successful union of nature with the art of man, in order to make her contribute to the wants and happiness of the human family."

In 1826 the population reached twenty-three hundred and here were all the conditions for the training of character. A small population, all known to each other, nearly enough upon a level to be animated by a common sympathy. all laboring for a livelihood, and therefore industrious in habits and simple in manners, no one could live in such a community without special incitements to a love of order and public spirit. And when from the inconvenience of four miles distance from Chelmsford post office and town meetings, those parliaments as they have been called for the free discussion of all questions touching the interests of the people and organs of popular communication with their rulers, the new town was incorporated, the election of its officers was with singular unanimity, a body of representative men—Nathaniel Wright, Samuel Batchelder and Oliver M. Whipple as selectmen, one of whom only survives, laden with years and honors.

In marked contrast to the town election was the city election, ten years later. The population in the territory having increased from 200 to 17,633 in sixteen years, the strife of political parties was never more angry, which resulted in placing in the Mayor's chair the amiable and talented Bartlett, whose vindication of Lowell operatives, if he had never written anything else, would entitle him to the gratitude of every Lowell citizen.

The age in which we have been privileged to live, is indeed a wonderful one, for within our half century, in common with the whole civilized world almost, we glory in the invention of the cotton gin, the railroad, the electric telegraph, the ocean cable and the use of anæsthetics for the abolition of pain.

When many of us came here, we had a weekly mail from Boston, brought on horseback from Billerica. Soon after an enterprising stage company took us to Boston in four hours; and the Middlesex Canal boat in five hours; and now, in that length of time, an answer by telegram can be had from the remotest city in Europe. Look now at our magnificent mills with eight hundred thousand spindles, and read the experience of one of our old residents, now present with us to-day:

"I was one of five small children, the oldest not eleven years old. We had cotton brought to our house by the bale, to pick to pieces and get out the seeds and dirt. We children had to pick so many pounds per day as a stint. We had a whipping machine made four square; and about three feet from the floor was a bed cord run across from knob to knob, near together, on which we put a parcel of cotton, and with two whipstocks we lightened it up and made it ready for the card."

Indeed, we old residents seldom have a meeting at which similar contrasts are not elicited.

Our career of progress and prosperity thus reflects the lustre of sagacity upon the founders of our city. It does more. To them belongs the honor of a high moral purpose. They were determined Lowell should not be a stain on the fair fame of our Commonwealth. For this purpose they established a wise system of business, and by various means in their power fostered good order, temperance, purity, schools and churches, intending to make the city an honor to Massachusetts, and a model to other manufacturing villages which might rise up. "Their works praise them in the gate."

No large portion of the population of New England, commercial or rural, has enjoyed more of the substantial comforts of life, and, on the whole, better intellectual and moral advantages, and long may the place be worthy of the title given it by Edward Everett, in his memoir of Francis Cabot Lowell, from whom it derives its name, "The Noble City of the Arts."

The triumphs of our city and its many causes of self glorification for the last fifty years must be left to younger voices. And now, in taking our farewell of the last semi-centennial we older men shall ever see, allow us to say in fifty years we have grown materially great and developed vast resources and improvements. We can show our visitors our immense factories and machine shops filled with the most perfect machinery, our broad streets, our palatial school houses, our handsome churches, our magnificent water works. But there are other things which we ought to show; we ought to show that a self governed and free people can be a power and example for all good upon the earth.

Let those upon whom the destinies of the city now devolve, see to it that that power of moral prestige which once made the young town so attractive in the esteem of our neighbors be not forfeited and lost.

"The country," says one of our public men, "will in a few months resound with eulogy of those who had founded the Republic; but those old patriots, if they could, would tell us to spend a little less in our efforts in praising them and a little more in following their example."

The President.—I have been endeavoring to prevail upon our old Grammar School master, Seth Pooler, to come upon the stand, but he says he will not come. I know you will be glad to hear from one who was associated with Lowell for several years as pastor of one of our churches and therefore I introduce to you the Rev. Dr. Miner.

ADDRESS

By Rev. A. A. Miner, D. D.

I am devoutly thankful, fellow citizens, for the honor and privilege of looking into your faces on this semi-centennial occasion. I recall a few reminiscences (I will not detain you long,) of the years from 1842 to 1848, when I was connected, as you have been told, with one of the churches here. I represented them, as I represent to-day, the heretical side of theology;—in theory now, in theory and practice then. And I found, I need not tell you, in the year 1842, and thenceforward, a very lively state of things in the theological world in Lowell. I had been immediately preceded by the Rev. Abel C. Thomas, whose skill and rigor as a christian warrior has but lately declined with the decline of his physical powers. He had been preceded by a gentleman whose venerable face I see before me, the Rev. Zenas Thompson, who had been mainly instrumental in the building of the church in which I had the honor to minister. There were gathered in that church, in those days, mostly young men and women, the flower of New England. I never spoke to a congregation which I more thoroughly enjoyed. Wide awake always. If I had ever seen man or woman asleep in that assembly, I should have believed that the stove was leaking gas, or that some other calamity was impending. We have been told to-day by the orator, that about everybody, in those days worked for day wages. I believe there was not a man or woman in my congregation who did not depend on his day wages for support. If there was any exception, it was that of the late Alexander Wright, Superintendent of the Lowell Corporation; and he, being a salaried man, was, I think, no exception. A noble man. There was in that body of men and women as much generous self-sacrifice as was ever found in any body of people of like means and resources. They built the church out of their own hard earnings. Whatever may have happened since, they never asked another man to pay their debts. They were men and women keenly alive to every demand of honor, to every demand of justice and of fidelity.

There were in the city of Lowell in those days renowned theologians. I recall the Rev. Dr. Porter, in the church near by; and the excellent Rev. Dr. Thayer, of the First Universalist Church. There were everal Methodist clergymen of repute here in those days: the Rev. Luther Lee, whose keen, sharp sword never had its edge turned, as he thought, the Rev. Dr. Blanchard, who has gone to his rest; the Rev. S. W. Hanks, of keen, incisive thought; and, I need not say, the venerable divine on my right, who moved as calmly then as now, and whatever were the theological strifes and encounters without, I do not recollect that a gun was ever heard from him outside of his own fort.

Those were days when almost every man and woman who walked the streets of Lowell, was alive to the highest interest of the city. You have heard much to-day on the subject of education, and having been entrusted during my residence here, with a brief term of service in the School Committee of the city of Lowell, I had the honor of meeting these two men, who have done more than any others to plant, fashion, mould, uphold and perpetuate the educational interests of Lowell. There was more than one warm discussion in yonder committee room. The six did not always agree in one; mostly however, in *two*. These men who were persistent (they will permit me to say) in their convictions, by the very inertia of that persistence, generally executed their thought; and if they even failed, it was because four were more than two. I look into the faces of gentlemen and of ladies who were teachers then, and some of whom are teachers yet in Lowell, I recall the name of the late Jacob Graves, who taught in yonder Grammar School, and whom I recollect of visiting for the first time as a member of the School Committee, when I was struck with the quiet and placid state of affairs in the school, the loving face that everything wore, with the beautiful penmanship that was exhibited, and with the very satisfactory condition, though apparently free from all constraint, that prevailed on every hand; and it occurred to me, while I was witnessing the progress of affairs, that I once had a teacher by the name of Graves in Franklin, New Hampshire,—a sub-teacher under Prof.

Tyler in the Academy there, when I was a lad of sixteen or seventeen. A second thought reminded me that he was an excellent penman; and I turned and looked at the master, and the impression stole over me, and grew more and more authoritative with me, that he must be the same man. In the remarks which I made at the close of the exercises, I spoke to the school of the very pleasant state of affairs, the genial aspect which everything wore, and the gratification I had felt in the exercises of the school; and remarked to them that it recalled a teacher of whom I had some knowledge many years before, that my teacher was a good penman, as was their's; he was a very genial man as was theirs; and it might strike them as a singular co-incidence that his name was Graves, as was theirs; and if I was not greatly mistaken, although the thought had never dawned upon me until within the hour, their teacher and my teacher was the same man. I then turned to Mr. Graves and asked him if he was not an assistant with Prof. Tyler at the Academy in Franklin, N. H., such a year, and he said that he was, but it had never occurred to him that I was a pupil in that school. It was a pleasant surprise to us both.

I have never ceased to remember with affection and admiration the faithful toil of the men and women whom I knew as teachers in Lowell; and when I come to appreciate the comprehensive judgment the wise thought, and the high skill, of the venerable men who helped to found and shape the schools, and who have watched them from the beginning until now, I am not at all surprised that the schools of Lowell stand unexcelled, not to say unequalled.

I remember Lowell, too, as a community awake to every moral interest. I think I may safely say I have never known a people anywhere more keenly alive, or more prompt to respond, to suggestions touching the moral welfare of the community than the people of Lowell at the period of which I speak. There are gentlemen in this city,—I see one before me now,—with whom I used to toil in the temperance cause. I do not know but that since that hour, one or the other of us, I will not to-day undertake to say which, has fallen from grace, but as we are foreordained to be saved, I think whichever it is, he will be recovered.

I remember, too, in those days of anti-slavery conflict, how a neighboring hall (for this hall did not then exist), used to ring with the discussions upon that subject. I recall especially one memorable occasion there, when a series of resolutions was offered that would seem to annihilate the American Union and the American Church at a dash; such as—First,—The church of Christ,—like its Divine Head, is, and ever was, opposed to all iniquity, injustice and wrong. Secondly,—Any church not thus opposed to all iniquity, injustice and wrong, is not a branch of the church of Christ, but a spurious and rival combination. Thirdly,—The American Church, judged by this standard is a spurious and rival combination; and it therefore becomes, a Christian and patriotic duty to seek its utter and entire overthrow. That seemed to be perfectly logical and conclusive. After two days of hot conflict, the clergy having been charged with being "dumb dogs," for allowing the church to be thus excoriated without daring to reply, a clergyman went upon the platform and said : " The first proposition is not true. The church of Christ is not, and never was, " like its divine head," opposed to all iniquity, injustice and wrong. It has always been charged with delinquency and unfaithfulness. Even the Apostolic churches, by this logic would be overthrown. Some of them, like the church at Corinth, were charged with sins not even named among the Gentiles ; and the seven churches of Asia are all described as lukewarm and defective in one way or another. The church of Christ is not and never was entirely and thoroughly like its Divine Head ; but it is and always has been aiming to *become* like its Divine Head." And so the stormy debate rolled on. It was alleged that at the last moment, when there was no opportunity for reply, a defence of the church was being made. It chanced that the parish committee of the church yonder was in session at that time. A message was sent to that committee asking that the church might be put at the command of its pastor the next day; and when a speaker from the platform alleged that the clergy were unfair, knowing the hall could no longer be had, and challenged them to open their churches and continue their defence, it was announced that that church would be open the following day, and the discussion be continued. Such were some of the stormy discussions of those days.

Now one word as to the inference which I draw from the example of the people of Lowell, and I will relieve you. When the civil war broke out, you all know how Lowell distinguished herself, under the lead of the orator of the day. The first bloodshed in the conflict was shed by Lowell men in the streets of Baltimore, and Lowell men were the first to arrive in the city of Washington for the defence of the national capitol. A few weeks before, when it was apparent that war was inevitable, in conversation one evening with two of the most wealthy merchants of Boston, one of whom, still living in ripe old age, being foreign born, and educated under the influences of the East, a noble man, in a tone of utter despair, said, " oh, your country will go to ruin. Your government is no government; it exists only on paper; it has no strength, and a rebellion of this magnitude cannot be controlled. We may as well give it over; for, look you," said he, "what can you do with populations like that of Lowell, where dividends will control the capitalist, where the need of daily bread will rule the operative, and where, therefore, you can have no support, no power." I said to this noble man, "I have had the honor to live in Lowell six years, and I believe there are no people on the face of the earth whose hearts will respond more promptly to the call of duty, or who will follow more quickly the impulses of high Christian patriotism, than the population of Lowell. I do not believe that our government is one of paper merely. I believe that it is a government that stands behind more bayonets, in proportion to population, and is backed by more Christian patriotism to-day, than any king on the face of the earth can boast of." How grandly these statements were verified you all know.

POEM

By John S. Colby.

"If this counsel or this work be of men, it will come to nought But if it be of God, ye can not overthrow it."—*Books of Acts, v* 38, 39.

I.

"Arms do I sing!" the Latin poet* cries,
And in majestic measure to our eyes
Unfolds the glittering panoply of wars,
The deeds of blood-stained heroes, and their scars.
Full oft have other poets, small and great,
Called down the Muses from their lofty state,
Lines to indite with crimson-colored pen,
To chant sweet strains and drown the wail of men.

Not thus to-day would we implore their aid;
Better, by far, the task alone essayed

---
* Virgilius.

In mortal weakness, without heavenly fire,
Our hearts to quicken and our tongues inspire.
Yet one there is among the Sister Nine
Whose melody is none the less divine—
Thalia called—in whom dwells kindly love—
A gentle daughter, sprung from Thundering Jové.

Her would we seek to be a guest this day,
And with her potent influence grace our lay.
Not then shall martial sounds engross our mind ;
But, with our grateful thoughts toward Heaven
     inclined,
The angel host our very souls shall thrill
With the glad message—" Peace on earth! Good
     will!"

II.

An Eastern legend, writ for childish ear,
Relates (what you will scarce believe, I fear)
That there was once a mat of virtue rare,
Which swiftly bore its owner through the air
For countless leagues, o'er river, mountain,
     sea,
Concealed from others, and from danger free.

A richer prize than this we all may claim,
And Memory, void of magic, is its name.
With speed of thought it bridges over time,
And wafts us gently to another clime.
I pray you, now, embark upon its wings
And backward fly, till into sight it brings
The mysteries of Fifty Years Agone,
When into life this goodly town was born.
Review, with me, the hallowed scenes of yore,
Assured that none the journey will deplore.

III.

When the ancient Roman mother held her child
     upon her knee,
Him she taught to worship Jove and "Father
     Tiber" reverently.

Prostrate falls the pagan Hindoo on the mighty
Ganges' banks;
From it earthly blessings craveth, to it render-
eth his thanks.
Egypt's swarthy sons and daughters homage
paid to sluggish Nile,
As the Christian seeks devoutly for his Heavenly
Father's smile.
And, although these sacred honors our unsen-
tient streams must lack,
Yet the welkin loud shall echo of the lordly
Merrimack;
Ring, the skies, with shouts exultant for the
placid Concord's tide;
For Lowell is the natural offspring of this hap-
py groom and bride!
Thus, while we, with hearts o'erflowing, cele-
brate our Jubilee,
They together softly gliding whisper of us to
the sea;
Proudly boast us as their best-loved, yet forget
not as they sport
Their three other buxom daughters—Lawrence,
Haverhill, Newburyport.
Children these of whom they well may quote
Cornelia's fond reply:
"These our jewels are, O Nations! Lucre
these could never buy!"
Filial gratitude return we! May their life-blood
never cease,
And the passing years bring nought to inter-
rupt their wedded peace!

IV.

"Glorious things of thee are spoken, Zion, City
of our God!"
Sang the Psalmist in his rapture, as famed Salem's streets he trod.
And as we shall scan the features of the sturdy
little band
Who with patience laid foundations here forev-

ermore to stand,
Start those words with honest impulse, unrestrained by doubts or fears,
As with fadeless bays we crown them, withered not by lapse of years.
They upreared no splendid Temple, such as David's vision viewed;
Offered up no sacrifices; reveled not in plenitude.
They built not around our borders mural walls of massive stone,
Nor the Presence of Jehovah claimed to be with them alone;
But with humble, modest labor sought to benefit their race,
Quite content if fickle Fortune did not wholly hide her face.

" Beautiful for situation, joy of earth shall this be called!"
Was the language of their firm faith, by no obstacle appalled.
Ay! if he has earned our tributes who has caused from earth to spring
Only one slight blade of grass, in spot where erst was no green thing,
Think you not those men and women have eternal praises won
That shall swell in future ages and the conqueror's fame outrun?
Priest and Prophet, Sage and Warrior, each may win a wide renown,
But he earns a nobler pæan who in peace doth plant a town!

V

No demi-god, or nursling of the wolf,
　Laid deep and strong the bases of our homes;
We burn no incense to their memories;
　No mausoleum towers above their tombs;
No sculptured column tells their gallant deeds
　In glowing verse, to heedless passers-by;

But on our walls their graces are inscribed,
   And from our hearts their names shall never
      die.

Who can forget the men who cast their all—
   Their art, their industry, their moderate
      wealth—
Into the balance of stern Destiny,
   And won her bounties not by secret stealth;
But with the brawny arm, the active mind,
   The consecrated soul and tireless will,
Strove here to bless their fellow humankind,
   Raising together Church, and School, and Mill!

Then laurels render unto HALE and BOOTT,
   To LAWRENCE, JACKSON, APPLETON and
      HURD!
Giants were they among the sons of men,
   And, like th' Apostles, grand in deed and
      word.
Let praise be sung to HOWE and WHIPPLE
      quaint,
To DUTTON, MOODY and their comrades all,
   To NESMITH, FRANCIS, WORTHEN, COLBURN:
      these
Shall future generations high extol.
Yet chief among them our godfather stands,
   Like Saul amid the Hebrew congregation;
And FRANCIS CABOT LOWELL'S name shall
      live—
   A household word and lasting inspiration!

VI.

Fast rose the structures of colossal size,
   Guided by men of genius such as these,
Till spindle, loom and shuttle ready stood
   To execute the mind's sublime decrees.
They dedicated not to frowning gods
   Their skill; no vestal virgins fed the fire
To satiate a mystic deity
   And turn away his dreaded, vengeful ire.
No! These were temples, but not futile ones,

MR. COLBY'S POEM. 79

To superstition nurse, and blind the soul :
Temples were they for man's advantage planned,
 And served by priestesses not clad in stole !
God dwelleth not in houses made with hands,
 When decked with human pride and vain display.
But wheresoe'er He finds a suppliant heart,
 And where *man's good* is sought from day to day.

VII.

To those who love the Lord, saith Holy Writ,
 And, loving Him, their brother-man do love,
All things shall work together toward good,
 And even seeming evil useful prove.
To-day our city is a monument
 That emphasizeth well that blissful faith ;
For though dark clouds have ofttimes lowered round,
 Onward and upward hath she trod her path.

From wilderness, where roamed the dusky band
 Of Wamesits, whom Eliot yearned to save ;
From rural precinct which the generous towns
 Of Chelmsford, Tewksbury and Dracut gave ;
From low estate as village, have we grown
 By swift degrees to city rank and station —
Proud of our history, our mammoth mills,
 Our maidens fair and — of our population !

When rang the tocsin of the dreadful strife
 That for a time armed brother against brother,
First offering made we for the Nation's life,
 And first foul Treason leaped our sons to smother.
But when Sweet Peace once more returned to earth,
 And sheathed the sword too long imbrued in gore,
None learned more quickly to forgive the wrong,
 And heal the gaping wound forevermore !

VIII.

Praise God! our Fiftieth Anniversary
　Brings no forebodings to us, of decay;
No deadly fever lurks within our veins—
　No slow consumption wastes our strength
　　　away.
Clear is our brain; our conscience free from
　　　guile;
　Our hands are busy as the tossing main.
We stand upon the very verge of youth,
　Eager a loftier pinnacle to gain.

The lesson of the Past we read with joy;
　Brilliant the retrospective view appears;
And, catching up the armor of the dead;
　We look with hope far into coming years,
Thus far the Lord hath bountifully blessed;
　Let this our confidence and faith enhance.
Placing our puny hand in His, so strong,
　Resound the word along the line—"Advance!"

LETTER FROM HON. SETH AMES.

BROOKLINE, February 24, 1876.

CHARLES COWLEY, ESQ., Chairman of Committee of Arrangements:

Dear Sir,—I find, greatly to my regret, that certain official engagements, which cannot be postponed, will make it impossible for me to join in the proposed celebration of the semi-centennial anniversary of the municipal incorporation of Lowell. To a man of my age, the recurrence of any special anniversary must have a serious aspect, but such an anniversary as this is of a peculiar interest. There will be few present at your celebration whose acquaintance with Lowell goes back to a remoter date than mine. It was there that I spent nearly twenty-one years of my life. It was there that my children were born. I there formed some of the most valuable friendships of my life, and I am proud to say that during my residence there I received not a few very gratifying tokens of confidence and good opinion from my fellow-citizens. In September, 1828, when I took up my abode there, Lowell was but a scattered and somewhat unsightly village. All was in promise and expectation, and I have often had occasion to reflect that among the anticipations as to its future growth and prosperity, those which seemed the most wild and extravagant have proved the most correct.

At that time, the whole of the east side of Central Street, from Frye's Tavern to the Washington House was occupied with a row of remarkably shabby wooden buildings, most of which have disappeared. There were a few houses on Chapel Hill;—on the north side of Merrimack Street stood the Episcopal church and parsonage, and two other buildings occupied as dwelling houses, viz: the princely mansion of Kirk Boott (which has since migrated to another part of the city), and the residence of Mr. Prince, which is still standing. Lowell Street had not been laid out, and the works of excavating the upper canal was perhaps half completed. Pedestrians, in going from Central Street toward the Episcopal church, usually made a short cut across what was then an open field between Merrimack and the present Middle Street. There was also a cluster of houses and shops in Belvidere, which was then a part of Tewksbury, and which, by its often defeated and often renewed efforts to be annexed to Lowell, furnished almost annual excitement, until the success of the project calmed all agitation.

I found the field occupied by five lawyers, not one of whom is now living, viz: Nathaniel Wright, Elisha Glidden, John R. Adams, Luke Eastman, and John P. Robinson. The principal business of a lawyer in those days was the collection of debts, and as the law then stood the body or the debtor was a sort of collateral security for the debt, and the number of suits for the collection of small debts was very large. The magistrate whom I found in possession of substantially a monopoly of that department of the judiciary was Esq. Hildreth, who lived in Dracut, and whose parlors often echoed the thunders of forensic eloquence. His docket was a very large one until another justice sprang up in another part of Dracut, who started a formidable opposition. Business was not so brisk with me but that I found time to receive the visits of a thin and pale looking boy, who was preparing for college, and came to me to recite his lessons in Virgil. That boy has since made some noise in the world, being no less a person than your distinguished fellow citizen, General Butler. If he should ever have the misfortune to make a mispronunciation, or false quantity in his Latin, he may possibly think that the fault was partly mine.

The rapid growth of Lowell, and its metropolitan position among the manufacturing places of New England, soon attracted to it a large number of gentlemen with their families from other places. It would have been difficult to find any other place in Massachusetts (Boston alone excepted), which furnished a more cultivated, refined, and charming society than was gradually collected in Lowell. Any man who lived on terms of friendly intimacy with such men as Pelham W. Warren, Luther Lawrence, Elisha Huntington, John Clark, John Aiken, and Thomas Hopkinson (one of the best men and best lawyers that I ever knew), might well be called a fortunate man. It would be easy to greatly extend this list of men, not now living, who were distinguished for public spirit and usefulness, as well as for private virtues and accomplishments. I might include some now living, but for obvious reasons of propriety, I spare their blushes.

But not to forget the old proverb that brevity is the soul of wit,— and that the indulgence allowed to spoken words may not be fairly claimed for expressions formally reduced to writing. I have only to thank you for your kind invitation, and once more to assure you of my regret that I cannot accept it.

I remain, yours sincerely,

SETH AMES.

LETTER FROM HON. JOSIAH G. ABBOTT.

6 ARLINGTON ST., BOSTON.
29th February, 1876.

CHARLES COWLEY, ESQ., Chairman.

Dear Sir,—I have delayed answering your note, inviting me to the celebration of the fiftieth anniversary of the incorporation of Lowell, hoping and expecting till this morning to be present. I find, however, I cannot be with you. I have been kept in the house for the last two or three days by a sharp cold, just bad enough to prevent my presence with you being any pleasure either to myself or others.

I regret it very much, as I had promised myself much enjoyment from the meeting, with those of my old friends and neighbors, who are left.

As you know, I have passed some of the happiest years of my life in Lowell, and with it are connected some of the pleasantest and best recollections of the past.

I took up my residence there soon after leaving college; there I married my wife; there all my children were born, and there repose the ashes of some of them, who so lived and died, that I am sure their native city has never had cause to be ashamed of them.

But my recollections of Lowell does not begin with my residence there.

Let me give you an incident which seem to me to mark the marvellous growth of your city. I by no means, now, reckon myself among the old men, and still when old enough to be permitted with an older brother to go off together some three miles to attend a Militia Muster, (Musters were then you know prime holidays). I recollect, we gave up the delights and attraction of the muster field and soldiers and their sham-fights, and trudged off some two miles further, to look at the beginning of the place which is now Lowell, and of which I had heard so much talk in all the country about. All I could see was one of the Merrimack Mills, the walls of which were partly finished, but all the surroundings were quiet and even wild enough, with only a few hundreds of people, where now you number fifty thousand.

The recollection of that visit in my early boyood, has always been very vivid with me, and at times it is difficult to realize the changes going on under my own eyes, in so short a time. It comes, to re-assure and comfirm me in the faith I have always had in the progress of our dear old Commonwealth, and her increase in strength and power. Your city, indeed, is one of the best witnesses, always before us, to the falsity of the predictions and croakings we have heard for years about the loss in the future, of that power, position and authority, Massachusetts has so far maintained among her sister states—I believe, and mean to believe that future is yet, very, very far off.

My acquaintance with Lowell began in the latter part of 1834, when it had a population, I believe, of about twelve thousand. I think all who lived there at that time and for the next twenty years, will agree with me, in saying that no city of its size, ever contained a more remarkable people, or a pleasanter or more cultivated city. I doubt if any place of as large a population, ever had within its borders a larger number of very able men, who would be marked and remarkable in any community.

The reason of it was, I think, that for some years our state had not been especially progressive or prosperous, but on the contrary, quiet and even languishing. Our lands, for agriculture, could not compete with the abundant fertility of the West. Our commerce had been paralyzed by the war with England, and was slow in recovering.

Lowell was the real beginning of a new epoch for our state. Here was an opening for men of energy, power and activity, who have been waiting for an opportunity—and it was improved.

At any rate, whether I am right or not in giving the true cause, I am sure I am right in saying that Lowell has had a larger proportion of thorough and able men in all the walks of life, than any place of the same size has ever known.

When you can point among your older citizens, who have gone to their account, to such names as Boott, Worthen, Moody, Colburn, Clark, Lawrence, Livingston, Huntington, Bartlett and many others of like position and ability, and to as large a number, yet among the living, quite as worthy and distinguished no one can well doubt that I am fully justified in what I have stated.

I have said the settlement of Lowell was the beginning of a new epoch, and it clearly was so, not only for Massachusetts and New England, but the whole country. It marked the time when we added another to the great interests of agriculture and commerce. Although we of couse had more or less of manufacturing in our borders, and experiments were beginning to be made on a somewhat larger scale than formerly, notably so at Waltham, still I think, Lowell fairly fixes the time when manufacturing began to assert its place as one of the great interests of the country. From that time it has gone on, increasing from year to year, at a rapid rate.

We hardly stop to consider now how fortunate it was that those intrusted with the establishment and management of the mills at Lowell were as wise, prudent and strong as they were proved to be. Although the manufacturing enterprises established there were really experiments, still they were so managed that not one of the large establishments promoted by the founders of the city, has failed, as I now recollect. They have had their ups and downs, yet have been able to go through all the panics and financial storms, without failing to meet all their engagements. No one can tell what would have been the effect on the manufacturing interest, just struggling for recognition, if experiments on a large scale had resulted in failure and loss, instead of reasonable success—it might have put us back for years.

But I must stop; I only intended to excuse my absence, and I am indulging in a great deal of gossip about the past. I could if I had time and you had patience, give you many other proofs of my statements that your city was always remarkable for men among its citizens of power, wisdom, forecast and patriotism as well. You were almost the first, if not the very first, to try the experiment of the then new system of transportation by railways, and as we all know among the very first to fully answer all the calls of duty to our common country in the darkest hours.

The history of the first fifty years of Lowell has certainly been marked, and one any city should be proud of. Let us all hope as the future is the outcome of the past, that at the end of the next half century her record may be equally good and brilliant.

Faithfully,
J. G. ABBOTT.

LETTER FROM SAMUEL BATCHELDER.

CAMBRIDGE, February 22, 1876.
CHARLES COWLEY ESQ.

Dear Sir,— I have received your invitation to attend the proposed commemoration of the fiftieth anniversary of the incorporation of Lowell, and I wish the state of my health was such that I could accept it, but I have kept my chamber most of the winter, only going out occasionably for a few hours in pleasant weather. And I am glad to learn that there are some of the old residents remaining who are better able to enjoy the reminiscences of fifty years ago.

Considering the facilities of communications by mail and telegraph at the present time, it would hardly be believed, that for the first year or more after the incorporation of Lowell, there was only a mail three times a week from Boston. Mr. Everett was then in Congress, and I wrote to him that it would be a great convenience to have a daily mail, and a change was promptly made to give us six mails a week, but so arranged that we had two mails one day and none the next. I wrote again to Mr. Everett, and he immediately had the matter corrected, so as to give us a regular daily mail.

The first establishment of a Savings Bank may deserve some note. After one of the Hamilton Mills was in operation I found that those in our employ suffered such frequent loss of their money by having in their boarding houses no safe place to keep it, that I allowed them to deposit it with the Company on interest, and opened a set of books for the purpose, on the plan of a Savings Bank. After a time Mr. Nathan Appleton suggested that it might be doubtful whether our charter would authorize this; I accordingly prepared a petition to the Legislature, for the incorporation of a Savings Bank. On receiving the charter I notified a meeting at my office of the petitioners and any others that felt an interest in the subject, to take measures for the acceptance of the act of incorporation. According to my recollection there were only five persons present, Mr. Colburn, Mr. Carney, Mr. Nichols, Mr. Beard and myself. It was suggested that if so little interest was felt in the matter, it was hardly worth while to organize; but Mr. Carney was willing to act as Treasurer, and we concluded to appoint ourselves trustees, and make the experiment. A few months after this the town of Lowell decided to build a Town House, and wanted to borrow the money for the purpose, which we decided to lend them. The sum, I think, was seventeen thousand dollars. This appears to be a very humble beginning for an institution whose deposits for many years past have been over a million.

With my best wishes that in future the institutions of Lowell may be as successful as they have been in the past.

I remain very respectfully,

SAMUEL BATCHELDER.

P. S.—I am tempted to add some reminiscences of more than fifty years ago, being a year or two before the incorporation of Lowell. I was at Boston in November, 1824, and in making some preliminary arrangements for the erection of the Hamilton Mills, before the company was organized, it was decided that Mr. John Lowell—who was afterwards the founder of the Lowell Institute—Mr. Nathan Appleton and Mr. Patrick Jackson should go with me the next morning, to what was then East Chelmsford, to decide upon the location of the mills. At that time there was no public conveyance through the place, except the stage to Concord, N. H., which started from Boston at four o'clock in the morning. Mr. Jackson and Mr. Appleton decided to go by the stage, but Mr. Lowell thought that instead of starting at that early hour, he would go with his horse and chaise the evening before, and invited me to ride with him. The subject of our conversation on the way was the plans then in operation in England, of organizing companies for working the silver and gold mines of South America. Mr. Lowell was of opinion that the application of English skill and machinery and English capital to the business, would make gold and silver so plenty as to diminish their value, and this appeared to be a very reasonable expectation, but instead of gold and silver becoming too plenty, or the parties engaged in those operations becoming wealthy, most of them become bankrupt, and neither those enterprises, nor the supply from California, have occasioned any diminution in the estimation of the precious metals, or been productive of more wealth than the cultivation of cotton in the South, or the manufacture of it in the North.

To return from this digression—which you will please to excuse, from "*narritive old age*" of over ninety years. We met the next morning on the banks of the canal, which had been excavated and the walls built, but the water had not been let in, and the only buildings on the west side of Central Street were two dwelling houses. The plans were laid out upon paper for four mill sites, between the street and the premises afterwards occupied by the Appleton Company. The Hamilton Company was the purchaser of two of those mill sites, with the privilege of taking two more within a certain time. On examination of the ground we concluded to take the two farthest from the street, for the reason that the elevation of the ground was such as would require less expense and delay in building, than those that were nearer the street, and we accordingly, on those sites built our two first mills. After I had been at Lowell some time I was satisfied that we had made a mistake in our selection, on account of the value of the land near the street, of which we had about four acres with each mill site, and proposed to Mr. Jackson, who was the President of the Company, that we should decide at once to take the other two mill sites, making a statement to show that the land would be worth more than we were to give for them, estimating it at seven cents per foot, besides the value of the water-power, which might be used on the other mill sites. Mr. Jackson thought I estimated the value of the land too high. However, we afterwards concluded to take the two mill sites next the street, and before I left Lowell, which was in about five years, we sold some of the land at fifty cents per foot. What the land on Central Street may now be worth, some of the people of Lowell know better than I do. S. B.

MR. B. W. BALL'S LETTER AND POEM.

Rochester, February 25, 1876.
Charles Cowley, Esq.

Dear Sir,—Your very kind letter of invitation to attend the fiftieth anniversary of the incorporation of the town of Lowell has been received. I regret my inability to be present, I claim to be one of the old residents of Lowell and am everywhere and always interested in her fortunes. Gradually but surely she is dilating into a great city, so that her second half-century, must surpass her first in growth and enterprise. But her first fifty years have been all that could have been desired or expected. Enclosed find some *impromptu* verses, commemorative of your anniversary.

Truly yours,
B. W. BALL.

POEM BY B. W. BALL.

A half a century ago
  Our mountain-cradled river,
Apparently had nought to do
  But just "go on forever;"
As it had gone since bubble-like
  Uprose New Hampshire's mountains,
Those granite water-sheds of rain,
  Which feeds its upland fountains.

Had nought to do but gash and flow,
  And leisurely meander
Till mixed with ocean round the earth
  Its crystal waves should wander.
Hydraulic engineers then came,
  And took just here their station,
Commissioned to henceforth arrest
  The waste of gravitation.

The awful squandering of force,
  Which bore with ceaseless motion,
The confluent waters of the hills
  From distant lake to ocean,
The indignant Indian stream they turned
  In part from its old channel,
And made its stainless waters weave
  Mere calico and flannel.

Old Father Merrimack withdrew
  In wrath into the mountains,
Veiling his anger in the mists
  Of his unsullied fountains;
And with him went his Naiads coy
  In haste to covert rushing,
To 'scape the lurid chemicals
  From smoking raceways gushing.

For like an exhalation sprung
    To life our first mill-city,
And year by year still louder grew
    Her shuttles' cheerful ditty.
Her prints outstretched the space would span,
    'Twixt earth and ring-girt Saturn,
For womankind in every land
    Have worn a Lowell pattern.

What numerals can e'er express
    The Milky Way of shirting,
To which the ginned, baled-cotton plant
    Her wheels have been converting?
For fifty years have turned about
    In many a murky dungeon
Her turbines and her overshots
    With plashing and with plunging.

The power-loom in her carpet-mills
    Has shown discrimination,
Like man himself the skill to make
    Artistic combination.
Whatever genius has devised
    To utilize the forces
Is working here to minister
    To human kind's resources.

Just fifty years, just fifty years,
    Have dreamlike flitted o'er us,
Since first within our gates was heard
    The Loom and Anvil Chorus.
Where else do fairer rivers lave
    A city, fairer, brighter?
Unto her exiled sons what sweet,
    Fond memories unite her!

No squalid, labor-hive is she
    Of hopeless, thriftless toiling,
Where gaunt, unguerdoned Poverty
    From morn till eve is moiling.
O'er Court and State and Senate too
    Her mill-boys have presided;
Her mill-girls oft, bewitching wealth,
    Through fashion's maze have glided.

With valor, eloquence have all
   Shed over her their glory ;
Her still brief annals boasting names,
   Which grace the nation's story.

Within her Campo Santo's* shade,
   Lulled by its gentle river,
Her youthful braves are sleeping well
   After life's fitful fever.

Thither in garments rolled in blood,
   With drums and bugles wailing,
The battle stricken forms were borne
   Mid arms and banners trailing.

There folded to his mother earth
   New England's Porson† slumbers,
Who knew as if his native speech
   The blind old Scian's numbers.

Softly the shadows of the trees
   His grave-sward green are sweeping,
Which through the watches of the night
   The starlight dews are steeping.
The Minstrel of the Merrimack‡
   Here once the muse was wooing,
From Belvidere and Dracut Heights
   The matchless landscape viewing ;

Here oft at eve with moistened eyes,
   Where earth and sky are blending,
Behind Wachusett watched the sun
   In fiery pomp descending.
While nearer rolled the glittering streams
   Through gorge and vale and meadow
Slow from their poet's glance withdrawn
   By twilight's deepening shadow.

LETTER FROM HON. NATHAN CROSBY.

Lowell, February 29, 1876.

Gentlemen,—Having a hard cold upon me I fear I shall not be

---

* The Lowell Cemetery.
† John P. Robinson.
‡ Whittier.

able to attend your proposed services at the fiftieth anniversary of the town of Lowell

As you kindly ask for any matter of local interest I may be able to communicate, I have thought I might perhaps contribute an item of historical importance in your reminiscences of the hour. I refer to the purchase of certain lakes and bays in New Hampshire for the greater security of constant water-power for the mills in Lowell and Lawrence.

The Merrimack River which furnishes water-power for our mills is the gathering of an immense water shed; the Pemigewassett branch reaching to the White Mountains and the Winnipissiogee branch to the Sandwich Mountains; the two Squam Lakes and Newfound Pond holding back the waters of the former, and Winnipissiogee Lake and the large bays in Meredith and Sanbornton, the waters of the latter. After the purchase of the water-power and lands now embraced in this city, surveyors were sent out by the new proprietors to examine the sources of water and to estimate the value of mill property upon the streams flowing into the Merrimack. While, as I have been informed, the report gave most valuable information, there seemed no immediate necessity or inducement to take measures to secure any water-power above Pawtucket Falls. But when about 1840 to 1845 mill powers here were nearly exhausted and some seasons of drought gave anxiety for the future welfare of the three large cities of Lowell, Lawrence and Manchester, the early ideas of securing the country reservoirs came up again in great force.

While living in Boston I had formed acquaintance with Mr. William Lawrence, and while conversing with him about certain mills in which I was interested at Meredith Bridge, located at the second dam below the Winnipissiogee Lake, he suggested to me that he thought it desirable for the Lowell proprietors to get control of that lake. I told him I was born in that neighborhood and had personal acquaintance with many of the people and thought I could give him useful information upon the subject. I subsequently made rough sketches of the streams, ponds, bays and lakes with the dams and owners of mill property and their probable value together with my views of water rights to be affected by purchase of the great reservoirs.

In 1843 I removed to Lowell, in expectation that the project would soon culminate in an effort to secure those waters. My correspondence was with Mr. William Lawrence only and private, which was continued to the spring of 1845, when Hon. John Nesmith, who had become largely interested in Lawrence, called upon me and gave me *carte blanche* to purchase the principal outlets of the large reservoirs and other water-powers below necessary to carry out our plan, and draw on Mr. Samuel Lawrence for funds. From this time onward Mr. S. Lawrence was my only adviser in the matter. I spent much time in examining the shore of the lakes and bays to ascertain what low farming lands would be drained or flooded by lowering or raising dams, and what property on the river would be affected in value by withdrawing or rushing along the water as the demands at Lowell might require. It was also desirable to make our widespread purchases as simultaneously as possible so that the fair market price of the property might not be disturbed. Careful examination of the value of each piece of property was, therefore made, and the asking price ascertained so that future complaint might not be made that the vendor had not received the market value of his property. When the preliminaries had been settled, various men were placed at different points and bonds for deeds obtained on the same day or within a few days, of the most important places. Many pieces of real estate in view of future accommodation and enlargement were bought afterwards. The purchases were made during the year 1845 and a corps of surveyors spent the winter of 1845–6 in surveying the amount of surface water, and we found one hundred and seven square miles of superficial water had been secured by the various purchases.

These purchases embraced the great lake Winnipissiogee, and both bays below in Meredith and Sanbornton, both Squams in Holderness, and also Newfound Pound in Hebron. The Hon. James Bell, a leading lawyer in the State of New Hampshire, and a very popular man, was a member of the legislature in 1846 and procured an act of the legislature, establishing a corporation of large capital, authorized to hold lands, water rights, &c., which gave all necessary powers to carry out the purposes of the purchasers. Mr. Bell became agent to manage the property and since his decease, in 1857, Hon. J. B. French of this city has attended to the very responsible care and improvement of the property. New dams have been built and in some instances raised in height, rivers have been cleared of ancient debris, flowage damages have been settled, and property at points resold or leased. Some three to five feet of more than one hundred square miles of surplus water are now at the command of the Lowell and Lawrence Mills— a holding back spring floods for us in summer drouths to the great benefit of every mill between the lakes and the sea.

NATHAN CROSBY.

LETTER FROM MISS LUCY LARCOM.

BOSTON, February 28. 1876.
CHARLES COWLEY, ESQ.,

Dear Sir,—It is inconvenient for me to attend the approaching semi-centennial anniversary; but your invitation calls back a crowd of memories from the banks of the Merrimack, among whose pine-trees and harebells my child-life grew into womanhood.

I see again the old North Grammar School, and the winding footpath that led up to it through a field or two—its adjacent cliffs and ledges, where we children found the breeziest of play-grounds—the schoolmates, now scattered wide apart, honored in their various callings and associations as they are loved and remembered by those who knew them earliest; and the teachers, who made the dreaded "public school" a place of happy occupations and intellectual conquests to so many of bashful, old-fashioned little girls. Graves and Pooler and Otis Morrill are the names of instructors I remember best, and many besides myself will recall them with grateful affection. Numerous are the men and women who will heartily testify to the merits of the school-system of Lowell, as an aid to their early mental development.

We who grew up in the "City of Spindles" in its younger days, should esteem ourselves fortunate in the influences that were thrown about us for good. The school and the church were more than nominal guardians and educators: they were like a friendly eye and hand following us everywhere. And those of us who worshipped at the old brick First Congregational Church must always feel that there the word "minister" held its full depth of meaning. We who knew him from early childhood as pastor and friend can only hear the name of the Rev. Amos Blanchard pronounced with profound regret for his too early removal from a city and a work he loved. A man whose sermons, rich in thought and piety as they were, by no means constituted his sole pastoral instruction—he acquainted himself with the tastes and mental bent of those who were growing up under his charge, and besides giving suggestions as to pursuit of special studies, he gathered around him the young people of his parish—such as were occupied during the day in the mills or elsewhere—for evening lessons in Moral Science, or for exercises in literary composition; joining them also in their social gatherings and excursions, as one who shared in *all* their interests. A scholarly man, of wide and deep sympathies and rare refinement—to be a parishioner of his, was in itself an education. And if this mention of him should seem to savor of personal feeling, it is a sufficient excuse to remember that Lowell herself owes him honor as one of her citizens, whose purity, wisdom and integrity entered largely into her history and character, from an early period. If the pride of a city is in the moral nobleness of her men and women, she should not stint herself in gratitude to those who by precept and example taught them scorn of any lower ideal.

My own relations to the history of Lowell is that of a toiler among her toilers. I began to do something towards my own support, by light labor in the mills, before I was twelve years of age ; living upon the Lawrence Corporation with my widowed mother, who had come to Lowell with her younger children, when the town also was yet in its childhood.

Work and confinement to close rooms were often irksome, but I had spirits and hopefulness, and many outlooks towards better things, through books, and friends, and Nature; and I think I grew up without any sense of hardship in my lot. In its later years, I became a contributor to the " Lowell Offering," and in that connection formed valuable companionships, and more than one life-long friendship.

Altogether, I am happy in claiming Lowell—not as the place of my birth—and I left it while I was yet a girl—but as my childhood's home, and the scene of my earliest growth into the struggles and the joys of living. Fourteen hours of labor every day was too much ; but we were intent upon making the most of our scanty leisure ; lectures and libraries and evening schools were well patronized ; and our occasional holidays were the more delightful for their rarity.

In looking back, indeed, it seems to me as if Lowell must have been a picturesque and beautiful town in its youth. What if its corporation-enclosures did wear an arid newness of sand brick ? They were in the midst of open fields, and in sight of the tree-bordered river, where now and then a wandering company of basket-weaving Indians came up in their canoes and encamped within a stone's throw of the mills; here and there a sod-thatched Irish cabin nestled in a hollow, apparently as much at home among the buttercups and wild geraniums as in the peat-bogs of the Emerald Isle ; and there were meadows full of violets all around, which even mill-children had time to gather, when the spring-freshets stopped the wheels ; the ledgy cliffs at Pawtucket Falls were a paradise of blossoms in May and June ; there were miles of winding canal, that on holidays tempted young feet into long, sunny wanderings through green pastures ; and there was the lazy Concord, loitering under oak and willow on its way to the swift Merrimack—the busy, beautiful stream that rippled an accompaniment to the young city's manifold song of labor, as it hastened onward to the sea. Never were there such sunrises as we sometimes went to meet, before the day's toil began, down the rocky bend of the river at Belvidere Village; never such sunsets as we saw from the mill-windows, burnishing the broad mirror of the Merrimack, and touching tenderly the few home-roofs scattered along the forest-crowned heights of Dracut.

Who among us thought of hard work as a trial or a curse? It was the New Englander's natural inheritance—it was the law of the universe—and as such was recognized and welcomed. There was ample breathing room, and no stifling population about us then. The glory of heaven and earth seemed to enfold us, as we toiled for our daily bread.

Inevitable changes have come, with years and progress. Better things are, and are yet to be, than have been. But I can think of no kinder wish for the children of the city which was the home of my childhood and early youth, than that their memory of it in mature years may be as pleasant as mine is to-day.

Yours sincerely,

LUCY LARCOM.

LETTER FROM REV. HENRY A. MILES, D. D.

HINGHAM, February 25th, 1876.

To CHARLES COWLEY, ESQ., Chairman of the Committee of Arrangements for the Semi-Centennial of Lowell.

Dear Sir,—Unable to accept your kind invitation to be present and to participate in the proposed celebration. I gladly comply with the suggestion, that, in case of absence, a letter may be sent " to be published with the official record " of the interesting event. I write the more willingly, as it affords opportunity to thank you for your kind remembrance of me, and to repeat, as I am always glad to do, the expression of my interest in the history of your city.

It is now forty years since I went to Lowell to live; and, though the last twenty-three years have been passed chiefly in Boston and its neighborhood. I have frequently re-visited your city, and so have kept myself informed of the stages of a growth which so early fell under my eye.

You will need none of my reminiscences to complete the picture of its rapid development, nor to set forth, what must be regarded as far more important than its material prosperity, the kindly, hearty, and high toned character of its people. The real marvel about the growth of Lowell is, that thousands suddenly brought together from all parts of the world, with no hereditary ties to that place, should so soon have become homogeneous, knitted together in neighborly and social offices, and made one people by warm fellow-feeling, broad charities, and a generous public spirit. A local attachment, which, in other places, has been the slow growth of successive generations, has here quietly taken root and borne fruit.

Much of this is due to the character of the men who gave the first impress to the place. I need not repeat names which will be on all your lips. They felt that the success of their enterprise turned on the hinge of making Lowell a desirable home; and, for careful sanitary regulations, for good schools, a high morality, an interest in intellectual and religious privileges, and an exclusion of all bigotry and intolerance, it soon took the lead of older communities.

Your celebration will be a day for renewing the past. You will be looking back and trying by the telescope of history to bring the fargone near. I may be permitted to turn that telescope to get a glimpse of the future. The good and honored men are not all dead. We cannot feel as did many years ago the prefect of a certain city near Rome. A commissioner of the papal government arrived, and, saying that he had a message to submit to the people, requested the prefect to summon all the best men of the place to meet in the public square of the city.

But, at the hour appointed, no one appeared. The prefect, being asked if he had done as directed, declared that he had. Being further asked where he had proclaimed his summons, he replied that he had gone into the graveyard, for, said he, the best men are there; read their characters on their tombstones, we have none among the living as good as those.

No one can look around Lowell to-day and see your recently introduced water-supply, your spacious school-houses, your well kept streets, your elegant residences, your prosperous churches, your charitable institutions, and the high-toned spirit of your people, without feeling that the present sons of your city are worthy of their fathers of half a century ago, and will leave, for the next semi-centennial, a record as good as that which you peruse now.

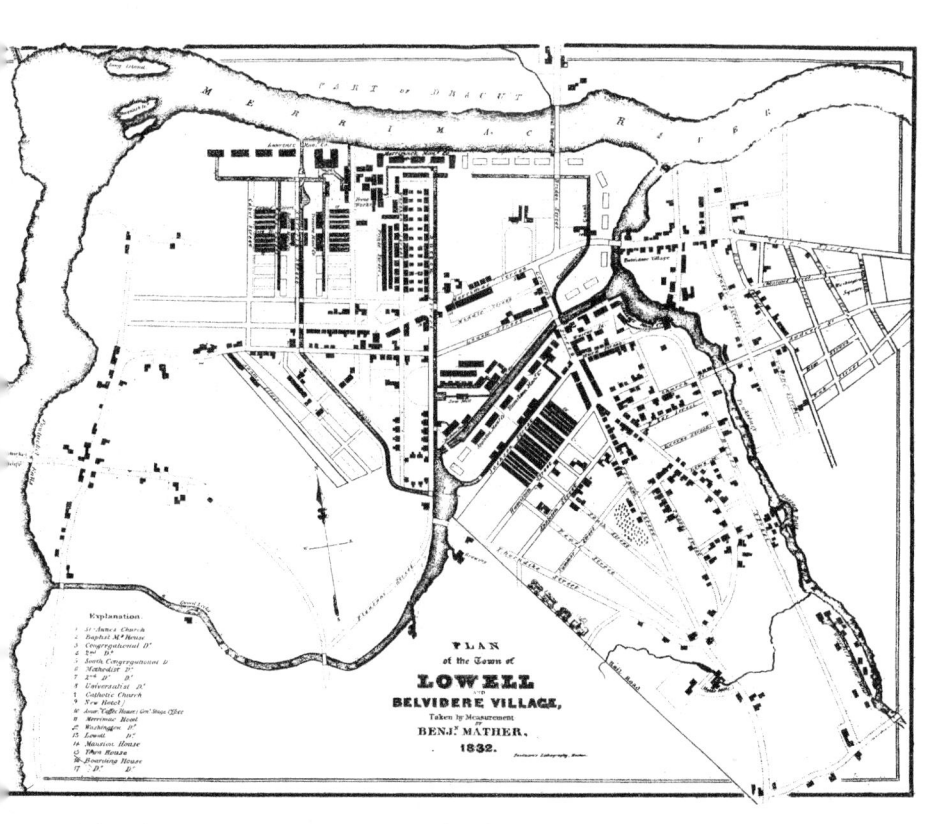

There are young men in your manufactories, there are boys in your schools, who will be the chief actors in the celebration fifty years hence. As they now see what a pure and strong current flows back to those who have gone before us, may they be inspired with the purpose to be themselves among the known and honored in the history of your city. Perhaps from among them will arise one, who, obtaining affluence by his industry and skill in Lowell, may wish to leave some proof of his local affection, and some token of his gratitude to the Giver of all good.

At the celebration of 1926 I think I see a grand, substantial, fireproof Public Library, bearing the name of some honored son of Lowell, and handing down his generosity to the latest generation.

What more precious monument of himself can any man erect? What a dear place will he take in the hearts of coming thousands! How eager will they be to learn everything of his personal history! John Harvard left not a large sum to start the college that bears his name! "I will give a guinea for every new word about him:" said the late James Savage.

A distinction not unworthy to be named with this, may be achieved by some resident of Lowell. All of us, actors and sympathizers in your celebration, will soon be forgotten, but his name may be repeated with affection many semi-centennials hence.

With renewed thanks, I am very truly yours,

HENRY A. MILES.

LETTER FROM REV. H. HASTINGS WELD.

RIVERTON, BURLINGTON Co., N. J.
Saturday, Feb. 26, A. D. 1876.

To the Committee of Arrangements of the Lowell Semi-Centennial.

Gentlemen,—Nothing would give me greater pleasure than to respond in person to your invitation to be present at the Lowell semi-centennial celebration. But my engagements prevent me. I have the heartiest good will toward the city—then village—in which I spent some of the pleasantest years of my boyhood;—and entered upon a nominal manhood, more boyish still.

But—the fiftieth anniversary!—That ordinal number has an ancient sound. When one goes to see his grandmother, he has the satisfaction of knowing that *she* is the oldest, and that *he* is the young fellow. He was not there when she was born. But, in this case you "Old Residents" are felicitating yourselves on the mature years of a city, the memory of which your memory antedates. And you invite me into the same confession. I would really like to see you, face to face, and note with what countenance you can conduct such an audacious proceeding.

I have had, within a year or two, the pleasure of comparing notes upon the spot, with one of the conspirators against chronology, who are trying to make people out older than they are. I have walked about, and ridden round your city of spindles. I have looked on old buildings (if anything grows old in forty years) the foundations of which I saw laid. I have seen crowded streets on the ground, for the "deeds of sale" of which, I printed the blanks. I have looked up at the windows of the real estate office, Gorham and Central Streets, second story, in which were conveyed the "lots," which, to the wise old men of *those* days seemed as North Pacific bonds seem to the cautious of *these* days. Now those same lots are held at a value which makes "Old Residents" sigh, in the words of the proverb: "If the old only *could!* If the young only *knew!*" We cannot speculate in vacant Lowell "lots" *now*. And we did not know enough to buy for investment *then*.

I might go into personal reminiscences; for there are many residents whom I remember. But to speak of some and not of all would seem invidious, and to mention all would be tiresome. I am writing this at the same desk on which I used to write editorials in Lowell, forty-four years ago. (Pray recognize the fact that there are some numbers below fifty). And before me lies, (it did not *lie* then) a volume of the Lowell Weekly Compend, for 1832. In its columns will be found a sonnet, written by one of the present Bishops of the Protestant Episcopal Church; and a notice that another gentleman, now also "in town," would debate, in the "Franklin Lyceum" with your correspondent. What a pity that all clerics cannot be Bishops! Perhaps I am too fast in saying this. In the Congregational churches "all settled ministers" can be Bishops and are. "Old Residents" will recall the names of the members of quite a goodly fellowship, who have gone out from Lowell.

Neither could all former residents in Lowell remain there, to graduate as "Old Residents," judging from the good work (of myself I say nothing) the emigrants have done elsewhere, of their going abroad we may remark, with Paul Dombey, "that's a blessing!" If, for instance, the vitality of your orator of to-day had been confined to the limited area of Lowell, a dynamite explosion would be nothing in comparison. The rest of us have worked, each in our way, some less and some more; and I think I may speak for all when I say that we look back with profit to our Lowell tuition, and with pleasure to our Lowell memories.

But I must not be prolix. Nor would I be *too* egotistic. For myself it only remains to say that your city motto, "Art is the Handmaid of Human Good," is the sum of what I learned in Lowell. In the editorial, and other inky entanglements, from which I have never been able entirely to escape, the truth there crystalized has been to me a clue in the labyrinth of political, social and economical discussion. And, in the higher vocation to which I have aspired, I have striven to teach that "to labor is to pray;" and to remember and enforce the fact that man was not created for idleness, but was placed in the garden to dress and keep it.

Accept my hearty congratulations on the growth and history of your city; and my special regards to the "Old Residents" who were the acquaintances and friends of the somewhat pert boy, (I fear) of 1831.

Yours respectfully
H. HASTINGS WELD.

LETTER FROM HON. E. C. PURDY.

SOMERVILLE, Feb. 28, 1876.
CHARLES COWLEY, ESQ.

Dear Sir,—Your polite invitation to participate in the semi-centennial celebration of the fiftieth anniversary of the incorporation of Lowell, was not received in season to enable me to attend; but I will not deny myself the pleasure of addressing you a few lines, if for no other purpose than to indicate the deep interest I feel in anything which relates to the history of your flourishing city. My residence there was comparatively short; but it was at an important era in its development, and was attended by circumstances which made a mark upon my own life.

In the fall of 1831, while residing in another State, I received and accepted proposals from the late John R. Adams, then owner of the Lowell Journal, to assume the editorship of that paper. At my earnest solicitation, Mr. Adams consented to publish a daily paper in connection with the weekly; and the "Lowell Daily Journal" was I believe, (though I may be mistaken) the first daily published in New England,. out of Boston and Providence. The name of the daily was subsequently changed to the "Courier," but I believe the daily publication has been continued ever since its establishment in 1831.

I was an entire stranger when I came to Lowell, and of course my work as an editor was attended with many disadvantages, and I did not feel, on the whole, that it was a success; but nevertheless, the recollection of the unfeigned kindness of some, and the encouraging indulgence of others, in the difficulties that beset my path, even at this late day, crowds fast upon my mind, and claims a grateful return, which I have too great a poverty of language to express.

I continued to edit the Journal for Mr. Adams for one year, at the end of which time I leased the establishment and published the paper on my own account. Before the expiration of my lease, however, the establishment was purchased by John S. Sleeper, Esq., (afterwards editor of the Boston Journal, and who " still lives," "full of years and honors,") and he, in conjunction with Mr. H. Hastings Weld (who then published a small paper in Lowell called the "Compend" continued to publish the Journal, daily and weekly, for a space of time, the length of which I do not now recollect.

At the time of my residence in Lowell, it probably held as bright an array of legal talent, as any other town of its size could boast; but of all its then resident lawyers, only the venerable John A. Knowles remains. Of the then resident clergy, only the much respected Rev. Theodore Edson continues to point out the way of life. Of a worthy host of physicians, I believe only Dr. John O. Green remains. Dr. Jacob Robbins, is, I believe, the only druggist of that time who survives; while Hapgood Wright, Esq., alone speaks for the continuity of boots and shoes. Not a dry goods man, or a grocer of that day now remains in Lowell, to my knowledge. The American House was then kept by Ira Frye; the Washington Hotel by Daniel Mixer; the Lowell Hotel on Gorham Street, by A. P. Blake, and the "Stone House" near Pawtucket Falls, by Major Coburn. Neither of these landlords can keep a mundane hotel. Of the general business men, Jona Tyler, J. B. French, and a very few others, remain to tell the tale of Lowell's early history. Their worthy *confrères* have gone—

"Some to the shades of the sylvan west,
  Some to the pathless deep,
And *more* to the land where the weary rest
  In their shrouded and dreamless sleep."

MR. PURDY'S LETTER.

At the time of my residence in Lowell, politics ran high. The "national republicans," (who subsequently took the name of "whigs") were a majority; but there were some disturbing elements in the party which rendered it exceeding hard to "manage." The democrats were a unit under the leadership of the late Rev. Eliphalet Case, who possessed many qualifications for a successful political "strategist." The fight in the old Essex North Congregational District between the Cushing and Anti-Cushing elements of the dominant party was bitter beyond all expression; and when Lowell was added to the district in 1832, the burden of the fight there, owing to the lukewarmness or positive opposition of most of the leading men of my own party, fell upon my own shoulders; and I do not know that I ever enjoyed a political triumph like that when Lowell gave a handsome majority for Caleb Cushing over *both* his competitors.

Perhaps two of the most notable incidents of my time in Lowell, were the visit of President Jackson in 1834, with the "three miles of girls," all dressed in white, who paraded for his reception; and the subsequent visit of the famous Davy Crockett of Tennessee, who also had a "reception," but in quite a different style.

But I begin to fear that the "garrulity of age" is upon me, and I will therefore close this hastily penned contribution to the general fund for your celebration, which I hope will receive many larger and better contributions from better if not *older* cotemporaries.

Truly yours
E. C. PURDY.

LETTER FROM HON. WILLIAM A. RICHARDSON.

COURT OF CLAIMS CHAMBERS,
WASHINGTON, D. C., Feb. 22, 1876.

CHARLES COWLEY, ESQ., Chairman, &c., &c.

My Dear Sir,—Your note of the 5th inst., inviting me to attend the commemoration of the fiftieth anniversary of the incorporation of the town of Lowell is received and I regret exceedingly that my official engagements here will prevent me from being present on that interesting occasion.

Lowell seems to have representatives in almost every part of the United States from among those who were formerly its citizens at some period of their lives. This fact has been forcibly impressed upon me during the past six years by so frequently meeting persons who formerly resided there, attracted here to the capital, from different parts of the country by official duties, business or pleasure. And when I was passing through San Francisco last summer an old gentleman who had lived there nearly thirty years and whom I had never seen or heard of during that time, called on me because he knew me in Lowell when he previously resided there, and because he wanted to learn something of the present condition of the city and of the people with whom he was formerly acquainted.

I may truly say I have never known a person who once resided in Lowell who did not ever after keep up, to a considerable extent, his interest in the city, however long he may have been separated therefrom by time, or however far he may have been removed by distance, and who did not look back with attachment and affection upon the place of his early residence.

I am very truly yours. &c.,

WILLIAM A. RICHARDSON.

LETTER FROM HON. BENJAMIN DEAN.

BOSTON, February, 22, 1876.

CHARLES COWLEY, ESQ., Chairman of the Committee of Arrangements.

Dear Sir,—I thank you for your kind invitation to join with the City Government and the old Residents' Historical Association in commemoration of the fiftieth anniversary of the incorporation of the town of Lowell. It is true that it reminds me that I am reckoned one of the old inhabitants, and among those whose youthful and frisky days are supposed to be things of the past; still the remembrance of those days is most pleasant, and, if we cannot live them over again in fact, we can live them over again in memory, which is the next best thing.

I came to Lowell a lad, about the year 1830, and being fonder of wandering in the woods, and paddling boats upon the Merrimack and Concord, than of wandering and paddling through books, there is scarcely a copse, cove, or glen in or near your city that is not associated with some romantic incident or exploit. That those incidents were not without pain and labor, no one better than you can appreciate when I tell you that, having bartered for a birch canoe with a travelling Indian, for which I exchanged·a rifle, I read Kidd on Corporations on those little sand-islands at the foot of Hunt's Falls. I used to run the rapids, and then lying full length on the sand, read twenty pages, and pole the canoe back again. I really believe that nothing but that best of all sauces, the exhilaration of a run over the rapids, could have made so dry a book palatable. The Hon. A. P. Bonney has the book in his library and I have no doubt he will find between the leaves some of the sand of those islands. You see, I can say of myself, as has been said of the Indian, There I paddled the light canoe along your rocky shores, and there I wooed my (not dusky) but lovely maid, and of course whenever I roam "my heart turns in fondness" to those bright and joyous days. It does more than that, it turns with kindest sympathies to everything that belongs to or comes from Lowell. If I meet any person who ever lived in Lowell, I look upon him as a better and wiser man than other men, and I know the women are more capable, lovelier far than all other women. But you want something of local interest, you say, that is something historical. Well, I sailed from Lowell to Charlestown in a packet on the Middlesex Canal, on the day, as I understand it, when the Boston and Lowell railroad was opened to travel. I don't know whether my father took his family by the canal from motives of economy or because he feared to trust all that was precious to him to that new-fangled notion of a railroad; certainly he couldn't have chosen a conveyance more suited to the tastes of his boys. The packet was quite commodious, and it was very pleasant to lean over the bows of the boat as the horses drew her slowly along, and watch the silly turtles who never knew enough to dive until the boat struck their backs, when they scampered down below. I remember as we passed one bridge—one of the canal men shouted "We don't kill men on this route." It seems that one of the railroad employees who sat on the top of a car, as was then usual, as if it were a stage coach, was killed by coming in contact with a bridge. Whatever the canal advantages were, in that respect it didn't boast long, for the railroad shortly killed the canal itself.

The next thing that the railroad killed was the steamboat built by Mr. Joseph Bradley which plied between Lowell and Nashua; no, it didn't quite kill her, but as soon as the railroad had started its tracks to Nashua, the steamboat had to give up, not the ghost, but the route, and was drawn by windlasses from above to below Pawtucket Falls, on greased ways, such as are used for launching large vessels.

I remember very well how we boys used to watch her slow progress up hill, and sometimes we thought she went backwards. At this time Billy Wright (Hon. W. H. P. Wright,) one of us, who has since been Mayor of a city, wrote a composition about "Patience removing mountains," in which he said " if patience will remove mountains they had better hitch her to the steamboat." His advice was taken or they never would have gotten her below the falls, but they did get her past the falls, and she waited all winter and ran over the rapids below to the sea, and was run some time on the Hudson River.

But notwithstanding my fondness for out of doors, I had to work some, and study some, to earn a living in a bar composed of such lawyers as Edward Mellen, George F. Farley, Thomas Hopkinson, Seth Ames, Josiah G. Abbott, Benjamin F. Butler, E. Rockwood Hoar, Albert H. Nelson, Charles R. Train, G. A. Somerby and others too numerous to mention. Lowell seemed to attract the active spirits of the land, and to bring out the brightest qualities. I practiced law in Lowell for a number of years in partnership with James Dinsmoor, we both finally left, he to go to Sterling, Illinois, and I to Boston. Nothing has occurred and nothing can occur to diminish my attachment to the place of my happy youth and early manhood.

Very respectfully, your obedient servant,

BENJAMIN DEAN.

LETTER FROM HON. MOODY CURRIER.

MANCHESTER, N. H., Feb. 25, 1876.

CHARLES COWLEY, Chairman.

Dear Sir,—It is with much regret that I find it inconvenient to be present at the fiftieth anniversary of your municipal existence, to which you have so kindly invited me.

Many of the important events of my life are associated with the early history of Lowell.

In the year 1836, I first took up my residence in your city, and from that time to this I have watched its progress with pride and satisfaction. I have not been surprised at its almost unexampled development, both in its material interests, and in the higher adornments, which have marked its upward progress; for I saw in its early stages, elements prophetic of a brilliant future.

The men who laid the foundations of your institutions, were wise builders; full of faith and hope they dug deep and broad.

They not only erected factories, but they built churches, school houses and libraries; thus physical development and intellectual culture took root together; and the energy and perseverance of the pioneer mechanics have blended with the refining influence of education, in making Lowell what she now is in her strength and greatness.

But it was not alone in the *men* of that day, that I had hope of the future; it was in the *children* of the public schools that my greatest expectations were laid, and I have not been disappointed. Many days, months and years I watched the expanding buds of promise; and I have lived to see my fondest hopes realized in the distinguished and honorable positions which many of them have filled. They are the men and women that now fill the high places, not only at home, but have earned distinction in other cities and states.

The men of 1836 have almost disappeared from the stage of action; here and there a few linger amongst you; but, like the stars of evening, which hang low in the western horizon, they will soon fade from our sight.

I hope and trust that the men of the next fifty years will carry forward the great work that will be left in their hands, by those who have been, and are now, working out the destinies of Lowell; so that, when that *Centennial* year, which you and I shall not see, comes round, Lowell will be as famous in her manhood as she has been active and aspiring in her infancy.

Respectfully yours,

MOODY CURRIER.

LETTER FROM JAMES PAYNE.

LAWRENCE, February 10th, 1876.

CHARLES COWLEY, ESQ., Chairman of Committee on Fiftieth Anniversary of Incorporation of Town of Lowell.

Dear Sir,—Your invitation addressed to Edward Payne, to be present at the exercises attending the commemoration of the fiftieth anniversary of the incorporation of the town of Lowell, naturally came to me, my father and mother having gone to their rest many years ago.

My father transacted business in England, in 1826, for the Merrimack Company, sending out men and materials for carrying on the printing business in a more satisfactory manner than had then been attained. Early in 1827, Kirk Boott, Esq., visited England for business purposes, and at that time my father entered the service of the Merrimack Manufacturing Company.

On Mr. Boott's return, my father, mother, self, Mr. Prince's family and others accompanied him, arriving in Lowell about the first of May.

My first home there was at the Mansion House, situated near the Concord River, kept by my old and esteemed friend Capt. Jonathan Tyler, where I and my parents remained until a house was provided for us.

I think your committee will admit my claim to be considered *one* of the "Old Resident's" a good one. I know there are a few of those left whose friendship I have ever esteemed and it will afford me much pleasure to meet them on the day you name, the first day of March next.

Very truly yours,
JAMES PAYNE.

LETTER FROM REV. J. W. HANSON.

Office of "THE NEW COVENANT" }
CHICAGO, February 22, 1876.

CHARLES COWLEY, ESQ., Chairman,

Dear Sir,—It will be impossible for me to attend your most interesting celebration. It happens to be just fifty years ago, that I, a child of three years, first saw the young city, whose growth and fame have extended throughout the world, though it was not until six years after that I became a permanent resident of Lowell. From that date, 1832—onward, I grew with its growth and strengthened with its strength, having been an eye witness of its wonderful progress during my residence, which ended in 1848, and during my residence in its near vicinity till 1865. I have more acquaintances and frinds whose bodies are in your beautiful cemetery, than I have in all the world besides!

Educated in its schools under Masters Graves, Healey, Morrill, Hoppin, Hanscom, Clark and Clapp, a clerk in the Tremont counting-room for seven years, I feel indebted to Lowell for all I acquired between the ages of nine and twenty-one, and look back upon those susceptible years as the most important of my life in shaping my character and destiny. How well I know every one of the old landmarks, and indeed every acre for miles around, where, on holidays and during vacations I tramped with boyish curiosity and energy. I knew the haunt of every wildflower and shrub where now the cultivated garden or the mill or mansion stands, and I remember the old places and the "old familiar faces" that your city knew from 1832 to 1846 as I remember no others.

My Lowell associations were crowned by an unanimous election to the chaplaincy of the Old Sixth Regiment, with which I served through its last two campaigns, and on the expiration of whose service I left New England for the West.

I send cordial greetings to all who shall participate in the Old Residents' Historical Association, and deeply regret that I cannot be present at what would to me be more interesting than any celebration I can imagine.

Wishing every success to the occasion, I am

Yours sincerely,

J. W. HANSON.

LETTER FROM SAMUEL LAWRENCE.

STOCKBRIDGE, February 25, 1876.

CHARLES COWLEY, ESQ., Chairman of the Committee of Arrangements.

Dear Sir,—I avail myself of your kind invitation of the 5th inst., to send some memories of Pawtucket Falls and its surroundings, near which my early boyhood was passed, and the change is so marvellous that instead of a reality it seems like a highly wrought romance. At the confluence of the Merrimack and Concord rivers, was a village whose commerce was made up mainly from fishing for salmon, shad, alewives and eels, &c., in their season. It was frequented by purchasers of these for many miles around. At that time there was very little property in Middlesex county. It had one seaport, a suburb of Boston, very little commerce, no manufactures, excepting in families, no banks or insurance companies. One of the principal water-falls was occupied; in it were two short turnpike roads, and the Middlesex canal. The summers of 1816 and 1817 were so cold that a general belief prevailed among large classes in New England that the climate was permanently changing and becoming too cold to ripen Indian corn and some other vegetables. Spots on the sun were distinctly seen for many weeks each of those summers. Agriculture was at low ebb, and about this time there was a great emigration from this state but especially from this county (Middlesex) to Ohio and other western states.

By a most beneficent act of Congress passed in 1816, the apparent destiny of Middlesex was changed. Mr. Francis C. Lowell was the author of this act; through the influence of Messrs. Lowndes, and John C. Calhoun, of South Carolina, and against the votes of Senators and Representatives of this state, it was adopted. This act laid a high protective, specific duty on foreign cotton fabrics, and its effect was as apparent as the act of Moses in striking the rock.

The first evidence of its effects was shown in the wonderful place whose half centennial you are celebrating. In 1816, this country consumed two hundered and fifty-thousand pounds of cotton; last year seven hundred million pounds. In 1820 the lands where Lowell is were not worth over twenty dollars an acre. Within a year some of the same have been sold at the rate of four thousand three hundred dollars an acre. Middlesex county is rich in educational arrangements, by the establishing of Harvard College in 1636, and in having within her borders Bunker Hill, Lexington and Concord.

Regretting my inability to participate with you personally, I am most respectfully yours,

SAMUEL LAWRENCE.

LETTER FROM JONATHAN KIMBALL.

Dear Sir,—In complying with your courteous invitation to send some reminiscences of early life in Lowell, it can only be expected that I should state personal experiences and facts, since its general history and chronology have long been before the public.* My first home was a farm house, standing near a small creek that issued into the Merrimack, not far from the ferry that united Dracut and Chelmsford, where now stands the bridge that connects Centralville with the city proper. The house, long occupied by Mr. Bonney, was afterwards built upon, or very near the spot. The whole neighborhood was a pleasantly situated, and somewhat seedy farming and fishing community. To one whose greatest expanse of water had been a small pond of an acre or two, formed by rains in the pasture-land of his country home, the river that divided us from the factories seemed a " world of waters." I saw it for the first time in early spring, when, with strong,

*See Charles Cowley's *History of Lowell.*

deep flow, it filled its bed almost to a state of freshet, and, turbid with sand and spotted with driftwood, rushed toward the rising sun. I easily recall the wonder at first felt when my father left me standing on the shore and entering a wherry dipped lustily his oars for the opposite shore where lay the daily work of his life. At that time, and for many months afterwards, a long buoyant scow, capable of carrying the heaviest teams, was the only means for crossing the river. No steamer of to-day, parting for Liverpool or for Bremen, is half as marvellous a creation as that ferry boat. It had a revolving platform at either end, which was thrown out whenever the boat touched the shore, to land and to receive the teams and the travellers. A wire of large dimensions, spanning the river and firmly fastened to a stout post on both sides, ran over pulleys fixed in two uprights framed into the upper thwart of the scow, and by this the heaviest burdens were safely pulled across, fearless of the distant rapids below. I remember to have crossed in this marvellous conveyance several times, and that the ferryman's caution to me always was, " to let the wire alone ;"—a caution which older passengers, when in haste, did not always heed, as the Charon of this dark river was never in a hurry. He had a monopoly of the heavy business, and the weighty matter that he bore made him *waity*, if you will excuse the conceit.

You landed on a sandy beach, walked up a sandy road to the level, and passed along open fields, on the left fenced with rails to keep the road out, and on the right appropriated to the use of the prominent man of the rising village. Small buildings were erecting on Merrimack and Central Streets, and it seemed to me that all the world must be in Chelmsford,—so busy and hurrying even then was the present pushing city.

I suspect that my first "voyage" was taken with my mother; for I have shadowy impressions of new clothes that came along about that time, "that I might look like other boys," a motive, I presume, that has ever since made a tailor's trade possible.

One of my most dearly cherished reminiscences is that of excursions a few months later upon the calm, deep bed of the river. A Dracut man at that time without a "canoe," as the wherry was called, was not much. My father hired a house—he hired also a boat, and at the close of the day in summer, or on some attractive Sunday would instal me in the sharp bow of the "canoe," where I could trail my hands in the water, and himself take a seat in the stern, and quietly paddle the light craft far up the stream past the red factories of the "Corporation," from one of which, beneath its arched cupola, ever was pealing the saucy bells. I remember the notched banks, with their small, shrubby growth fringing the stream; the boats that lay fastened to a root by chain and padlock, shining some with newly applied tar, others in green, yet others as red as paint could make them; the tortoises that sunned their backs on some quiet log or rock, and the brotherly frog noisy, yet harmless, as croakers are wont to be when in their element. The usual place of landing was on the largest of the islands thrown up by the excavating power of the river as it left the rough declivities of Pawtucket, and inhabited by fishermen in the spring season, when their labors trenched upon the darkness. My early recollections of the islands, however, are of uninhabited sandy slips with stunted birches and alders, partially, even largely cleared, where one could lunch in the shade or bask in the hottest of suns. Here stood all deserted the rough fish houses with stone chimney, and a raised floor for the rude bedding or wraps used by the fishers. On the shore a large windlass with handles at either end aided to draw in the lines of the huge net that swept the salmon and shad from their retreats.

Though certainly unable to read a word at that time, from hearing others or from conversation, I had a kind of ideal knowledge of the great world as it now exists. The river was my sea; the islands rising from it used to impress me, as perhaps on the broad Pacific they do to-day the voyager long from shore, as very pleasant refuges. The canoe would be paddled from one to another, not always to land upon it, but to drop into the eddies below them, lie quietly and watch the different kinds of small river fish that glanced back and forth, or balanced themselves above their nests. There were times when our excursions may have extended to Beaver Brook, as I afterwards knew it, but of this I am not clear. It is pretty well settled, however, that my first recollections of the "Falls" were impressed by viewing them from below. I cannot recall the time when their roar was not familiar to my boyhood, and the ragged spurs that overtop the river at its usual stages of water, are, to-day, distinctive features of my Lowell reminiscences.

But I am sending you, I fear, a long and garrulous communication. It is the reproduction of the first boyish impressions I have of Lowell and the Merrimack. A few months subsequently I moved into the town of Tewksbury, into the village so fittingly named Belvidere, which in those days, as well as now, combined more natural beauties and attractions than all beside. From this locality you will hardly want the more mature recollections I could give you, however pleasing

it might be to me to drone them out in a leisure hour.
Very truly yours,
J. KIMBALL.

LETTER FROM THOMAS B. THAYER, D. D.

BOSTON, Feb. 21, 1876.

CHARLES COWLEY, ESQ.

Dear Sir,— I thank you most cordially, and through you the "Committee of Arrangements," having the matter in charge, for an invitation to the "Fiftieth Anniversary of the Incorporation of the Town of Lowell," to be celebrated on the first of March next.

Having spent so many years of my active ministry in Lowell, beginning with the year 1833, it would afford me great pleasure to be with you, and share in the rejoicings of an occasion which must be fraught with profoundest interest to all the early dwellers of "the town of Lowell." But after a careful review of the circumstances, I find myself compelled, though with sincere regret, to decline the invitation so kindly and thoughtfully extended to me.

As regards the "letter relating to matters of local interest," I can only say that my memories of early life in Lowell, and of incidents and events having any general interest, are, I suppose, a kind of common property; and will no doubt find far more eloquent and pleasing expression in the speeches of the day, than I can give them in a formal letter. The living voice and manner in this case are infinitely more attractive and potent than the pen.

And so with many thanks to the Committee and to yourself, and heartily desiring for all a delightful anniversary, I am very respectfully yours,

THOS. B. THAYER.

LETTER FROM WILLIAM S. ROBINSON.

MALDEN, Feb. 29, 1876.

MY DEAR MR. COWLEY,—I am sorry not to be able to visit Lowell on the fiftieth anniversary of the organization of its government. I had a plenty of impromptu puns and unpremeditated jokes ready to put to paper to-day; but they are now flatter than "Melvin's beer," which used to be made on Chapel Hill, and the "author" of which, Mr. Emerson Melvin, was one of the authors Concord contributed to the new place which popped into existence half a century ago, with a shot heard just half around the world. This linking of Mr. Emerson and Mr. Melvin together may be taken as an act of propitation by the Concord ladies toward the closing of the bottle of contention opened last April. I could tell you many good stories about the Melvin family, who had a wit " tough and screaming as birch-bark," as Concord people knew well enough, and Lowell people also.

But as I have no time now to write them, and as little talent, I am afraid, for anything else, you will have plenty that's reminiscential, as well as the more solid half-centennial solid from the old editor of the *Courier* and the *Tri-Weekly American*, who was tried and found wanting in Lowell a quarter of a century and more ago. I shall enjoy a reading of the good things.

With many thanks to the Committee, in behalf of Mrs. Robinson, as well as of myself, I remain,

Yours ever,

WM. S. ROBINSON.

The hand of death was already upon " Warrington" when the foregoing letter was penned, and on March 11th he expired. The widow of Mr. Robinson, soon afterwards, favored the press with a letter of reminiscences of her early life in Lowell, beginning in 1832. The following paragraphs are from Mrs. Robinson's letter:—

" Help was in great demand, and fabulous stories were told of the new town (formerly Chelmsford) and the high wages offered to all classes of work-people; stories that reached the ears of mechanics and machinists in all parts of New England, and gave new life to lonely and dependent women in distant towns and farm-houses. Into this El Dorado of needy people they began to pour by the various modes of travel known to those old days. They came by the slow-toiling canal, which then " traced its sinuous way" from Boston to Lowell. This canal is no longer used, and there is nothing left of it but a little spot where it began in Charlestown. There, any one going by the Maine Railroad can see, just before reaching the Somerville station, a few decayed willows nodding sleepily over its grass-grown channel and ridgy paths, a reminder of those slow times when it took a long summer's day to travel the twenty-eight miles between Boston and Lowell. The canal boat came every day, always filled with new recruits to the army of useful people. The mechanic and machinist came, each with his home-made tool chest, his household stuff, and his wife and little ones. The widow came with her little flock, and her scanty house-keeping goods, to open a boarding house or variety store, and so provide a home for her fatherless children. People with past histories came, to hide their griefs and their identity, and to earn an honest living by the 'sweat of their brow.' Single young men came, full of hope and life, to get money for an education, or lift the mortgage from the home farm.

Troops of young girls came by stages and baggage wagons, and men were employed to go into other States and Canada and collect them at so much a head and deliver them at the factories.

A very curious sight these country girls presented to young eyes accustomed to a more modern style of things, when the large, covered baggage wagon arrived in front of a 'block' on the corporation. They would descend from it, dressed in various and outlandish fashions (some of the dresses, perhaps, having served for *best* during two generations) with hair *done* up in (to us) almost impossible ways, and with their arms brim-full of bandboxes containing all their worldly goods. Here let me pay a passing tribute to that obsolute appendage to a lady's baggage—the bandbox! It has a New England history almost coeval with that of Lowell. It began to be made in perfection about fifty years ago in Jaffrey, N. H., by a woman named Hannah Davis, who manufactured the first *nailed* bandboxes in the country, and made herself rich thereby.

Another Hannah—Hannah More—always travelled with the immortal bandbox, besides her ' great bag, little bag, basket, bundle.' The bandbox was made of all sizes, many of them being large enough to hold quite a wardrobe. Now, the omnivorous ' Saratoga' has swallowed them all up, and it is my fate to chronicle the 'last of the bandbox.'

These country girls, as they were called, had queer names, which added to the singularity of their appearance. Samantha, Trifeny, Plumy, Elgardy and Florilla were common among them. They soon learned the ways of the new place to which they had come, and after paying for their transportation, they used their earnings to re-dress themselves, and in a little while they were as stylish as the rest; for they had good New England blood in them, and blood tells even in factory people. In time most of them changed their names to Mrs.——— something, and later, when Andrew Jackson visited Lowell, no peculiarity of dress in the operatives was seen, but walking four deep in procession to his honor, clothed in white, these Lowell factory girls looked, to use the words of a contemporaneous writer, 'like liveried angels.'

The first strike, or 'turn-out,' as it was called, was in 1836, and was caused, of course, by the reduction of wages. The operatives were very indignant; they held meetings and decided to stop their work and turn out and let the mills take care of themselves. Accordingly, one day they went as usual, and when the machinery was well started up they stopped their looms and frames and left. In one room some indecision was shown among the girls. After stopping their work they discussed the matter anew, and could not make up their minds what to do, when a little girl of eleven years old said, 'I am going to turn out whether any one else does or not,' and marched out, followed by all the others. The 'turn-outs' all went in procession to the grove on 'Chapel Hill' and were addressed by sympathizing speakers. Their dissatisfaction subsided or burned itself out in this way, and though the authorities did not accede to their demands, they returned to their work, and the corporations went on cutting down the wages.

Lowell, for a young city, has furnished a large number of distinguished men. Its first Mayor, Dr. Bartlett, was widely known as a man of scientific culture and of many accomplishments. The Daltons (father and sons), Dr. Kimball, the celebrated surgeon, and Lieut. Gov. Huntington also practised medicine there. Huntington is now dead, but in his day was no doubt the most popular man in the city. Wendell Phillips was in a law office there. John Nesmith, manufacturer, was also Lieutenant Governor during a part of Andrew's term of office. The most wealthy man in Lowell is Dr. James C. Ayer. In Free Soil days Whittier edited a paper, and John H. Warland and H. Hastings Weld were in the same profession. Mr. Warland is now dead. Col. Schouler began editorial life there, assisted by 'Warrington,' who went there from Concord, Mass., in 1842. 'Warrington' also published the *Lowell American*, a Free Soil paper, from 1849 to 1854. Wm. Worthen, of the firm of D. Appleton & Co., of New York, was formerly of Lowell, a Worthen being one of the founders of the city. Warren Colburn, of the 'Sequel,' was agent of the Merrimack Mills. John P. Robinson, who was so seriously lampooned, for no reason that the poet gives except that he was a 'he,' moved to Lowell from Dover, N. H., early in life. He was a man of Choatean look and complexion, extremely nervous, and a good lawyer. It is not necessary to say that Gen. Butler is now the most widely-known citizen of Lowell. Henry F. Durant, the founder of Wellesley College, studied law in his father's office, in Lowell, with Gen. Butler. Gen. Banks was a bobbin-boy and afterward editor there. Rev. W. H. Cudworth and Rev. J. W. Hanson, now of Chicago, are cousins and Lowell boys; they were both chaplains of Massachusetts Regiments during the war.

Lowell has never been a book-publishing place, but it is a curious fact that the American edition of *Hayward's Faust* was published there in 1840, by Daniel Bixby, now of New York."

LETTER FROM REV. FRANCIS MANSFIELD.

179 PARK AVENUE, CHICAGO, Feb. 28, 1876.

To the Semi-Centennial Committee :

Gentlemen,—My earliest recollections of Lowell go back to thirty-five years ago, when as a little schoolboy, I played on the bank of the Concord river, and strolled through the neat streets named after Lawrence and Tyler. I have abundant reason to remember the grammar school on Chapel Hill, where the famous Mr. Merrill taught the boys with ferrule in hand, and expelled at least one for the gross offence of turning round and whispering to another boy behind him. Much more agreeable, however, are the recollections of the grammar school on Middlesex Street, where Mr. Morse taught the elements of English education. Still more delightful was the instruction received at the North grammar school, under the amiable Christian gentleman, the late Otis Morrill. It was from this school that the writer entered the High School at the time when the fatherly C. C. Chase " checked" the lads for misbehaviour, and taught Greek Syntax from Crosby and Kühner. Under the faithful instruction of Mr. Young, we learned Physiology and Natural Philosophy. Mr. Farnsworth taught us Penmanship and Book-Keeping. The keen, quick-witted and sharp Mr. Russell, the Mathematician, gave us instruction in Algebra and Geometry, while the polite and accomplished gentleman, Mr. Kimball, succeeding Miss Sawyer as principal of the female department, still continued to be our professor of Latin, and took us through the orations of Cicero and the Æneid of Virgil. Once during the campaign of Scott against Pierce, while political partizanship ran very high, the boys of the High School, partaking of the spirit of their sires, arrayed themselves at recess on opposite sides of the walk, and the Whig candidate was elected by a two-fold majority. As this vote was taken previous to the election, it has ever been a matter of deep regret that the county did not follow their example, and endorse their decision Among my earliest political recollections, also, I may mention the distinguished name of the indomitable Butler, who, then a democrat, standing on the platform in the public squares or mounted on the rostrum in the old City Hall, fulminated his terrible denunciations against the Godlike Daniel Webster, the great Brahma of Massachusetts idolatry.

No one who had the good fortune to be present in the City Hall on one occasion, will ever be able to drive from his memory the recollection of the scene when a young Irish orator from Nashua, N. H., came forward, and was introduced by Mr. Butler, and began to speak for a coalition between Democrats and Free-Soilers in Massachusetts, during the year when Mr. Boutwell was elected Governor. Scarcely had the young man uttered ten words, when he said it was proposed to make this a "test question," referring to a religious test between Romanists and Protestants, implying that the Papists were on his side. Such a scene of uproar and confusion as then ensued, I have never witnessed, before or since. Hissing, groaning, scraping, hooting, all sorts of hideous noises, combined to drown the voice of the speaker. Mr. Butler, in an instant, threw off his coat in the heated atmosphere, came forward in his shirt-sleeves, simply waved his hand before the tumultuous and enraged audience, and in a moment all was so quiet that you could hear the ticking of the clock in the further end of the hall. Mr. Butler begged them to hear the young man speak, and promised that he would make no further allusion to the subject of the " test question." The young man tried to begin again, but the loud uproar was renewed, and the audience would not allow the orator from Nashua to utter another word. Mr. Butler finished the evening with one of his most eloquent and characteristic speeches.

I dare say that the memory of many old citizens of Lowell will recall the reception extended by the city to John Tyler, President of the United States, when he visited New England in 1843. It was a delight to the young lads of the public schools to march in procession through Middlesex Street and to stand in line along the old board sidewalk, a little east of the Brewery Hill, and gaze into the face of so august a personage, as he rode by in open carriage, with coachman and footman, escorted in grand style by the officers of the City government, accompanied by other distinguished persons. Imagine our wonder and gratification to see a real live president.

Another time of interest was presented to the boys of the public schools when William Livingston first opened the "new route" from

Lowell to Boston. The first time the cars went over the Salem route to Boston, we were invited to go and test the line. Furnished with excursion tickets, including admission to the Boston Museum, we were enthusiastic in admiration and praise of the trip which we took, and the performance which we witnessed, and returned to our homes extremely gratified by the excursion of the day.

It was also an extremely interesting occasion when the celebrated Dracut bridge case was tried in the new Court House, on Chapel Hill. Here Choate and Butler were arrayed on opposite sides against each other; the former being retained by the company, the latter by the city of Lowell. The arguments were among the ablest and most effective ever made by these distinguished advocates. The seats and benches and aisles were filled with the beauty and fashion of the city. Here Mr. Butler illustrated his argument by narrating the story of the man who took his friend out to walk in his garden, and the latter fell headlong into a deep hole in the earth, which had been covered with light twigs and straw, "Oh, said he, I meant to have told you of that hole." "Never mind" said his friend, "I have found it myself.' This reply was uttered by Mr. Butler with such inexpressible drollery that the whole audience and jury burst into laughter; and even the sober judge could hardly suppress a smile. Mr. Choate in replying said at the beginning of his speech, "I suppose I have as much right to be long and tedious as my learned opponent." Choate, as a matter of course, obtained judgment against the city for the bridge company; but the ability and eloquence of Butler, together with his shrewdness and skill in argument, served greatly to reduce the amount of the damages. The days of the young *Butler* who, as was publicly reported, did not treat the nose of Judge —— with due respect, but wrung it unmercifully while descending the stairs, because the latter decided a case against him in the Police Court:—the days of the young Butler had now changed.

I should like to add something of the history of the "Lowell Adelphi," the society which, in former days, brought to Lowell, at great expense, some of the most eminent lecturers of the time. Henry Ward Beecher, E. H. Chapin, Thomas Starr King, Dr. Clark and Judge Crosby were introduced to the citizens of Lowell in the capacity of public lecturers by this enterprising society, among whose members are many gentlemen who have since obtained distinction.

Very truly yours,

FRANCIS MANSFIELD.

LETTER FROM HON. ROBERT C. WINTHROP,

PRESIDENT OF THE MASSACHUSETTS HISTORICAL SOCIETY.

BOSTON, February 26, 1876.

CHARLES COWLEY, ESQ.,

Dear Sir,—I thank you and the Committee of Arrangements for your obliging invitation. I regret that it will be out of my power to unite with you in the celebration of the fiftieth anniversary of the incorporation of Lowell.

I dare not hope that I can contribute anything of "local interest," as you request, which is not familiar to you already. But I cannot forget that my valued friend, the late Hon. Nathan Appleton, in an autobiographical sketch which he gave me in manuscript, said of Lowell, that he might, perhaps, claim to have given it the name. The Act of Incorporation was ready to be reported. Nothing remained but to fill the blank with a name. Two names only were suggested, of which Lowell was one. "Lowell, by all means," said Mr. Appleton; and Lowell it was.

Nathan Appleton cannot be forgotten in any commemoration of the rise and progress of your city. No man did more *to give it a name*, in more senses of the word than one;—a name and a praise throughout our land.

Believe me, Dear Sir, respectfully and truly yours,

ROBERT C. WINTHROP.

LETTER FROM HON. JOHN. G. PALFREY.

CAMBRIDGE, February 16, 1876.

CHARLES COWLEY, ESQ., Chairman, &c., &c.

Sir,—The state of my health is such that I shall not be able to avail myself of the kind invitation conveyed in your note of the 5th inst. Below is a little memorandum of all that I have to say respecting the matter to which you call my attention.

Respectfully, your obedient servant,

J. G. PALFREY, by A. R. P.

In the summer of 1808—possibly it may have been in that of 1807—I went from Boston to make a visit of a few days at Mr. Gedney's house in what was then Tewksbury. I walked the latter part of the way, quitting the stage-coach, I believe, at Billerica. Mr. Gedney had, I believe, lived in Demarara, where he had been a friend of Mr. Gardner Greene of Boston. I understood Mr. G. to be an Englishman. His wife was an invalid, and seemed some years older than himself. They lived in the house which now makes part of the Hospital behind St. Luke's Church in Belvidere. Mr. Gedney was fond of fishing, and I have passed hours in a boat with him where the Concord empties into the Merrimack, taking what he (whether properly or not, I cannot say) called *Roach* and *Bream*. It was a perfect solitude. There was no sound of human life. And, unless my memory deceives me, no building on the south side of the Merrimack was in sight from the house.

LETTER FROM HON. JOHN K. TARBOX,

REPRESENTATIVE IN CONGRESS FROM THE LOWELL DISTRICT.

WASHINGTON, D. C., Feb. 26, 1876.

CHARLES COWLEY, ESQ., Chairman of Committee.

Dear Sir,—Duties here forbid my acceptance of the polite invitation you extend to me to unite in the public observance of Lowell's semi-centennial. But I give homage to the event.

You celebrate an achievement more honorable than the victories of war—as much worthier of renown than warlike deeds as the genius to create is grander than the skill to destroy. Lowell is herself a monument to the sagacity of her founders, and an illustration of American enterprise, rich in suggestion and instruction, which the distinguished orator of the occasion will not fail to enforce worthily. Her personal and local reminiscences, while cherished by her people, may not interest the world at large; but the fact of her existence, and how and why she exists, and her character as representative of an important department of the world's industry, make her history a not insignificant part of the history of all industrial growth.

I deem your commemoration happy from its coincidence with the great international event to which the nations come as guests of the Republic to exhibit on American soil the trophies won by civilized society in manufactures, the arts and sciences, and in every field of human effort. In the distribution of honors to those who deserve well for faithful work done in their generation, we should not lose from our grateful memory of benefactors and achievers the names of the Lowells, the Lawrences, and their honorable compeers. I am sure the good people of Lowell do but indulge a proper pride in their congratulations upon their career as a distinctive community. Therein they will give expression to the sentiment of neighborhood loyalty, which is the germ and nurture of patriotism. The citizen who could be false to his town might betray his country!

With thanks to the committee for their courtesy,

I am very truly yours,

JOHN K. TARBOX.

LETTER FROM HON. E. R. HOAR.

CONCORD, February 19, 1876.

CHARLES COWLEY, ESQ., Chairman of Committee.

It will give me much pleasure to accept the invitation of the Committee of Arrangements of the City Government of Lowell, to attend the exercises to commemorate the fiftieth anniversary of the incorporation of the town of Lowell, on the first day of March next, unless some professional engagement should prevent.

Even *half* a "centennial" should be treated with some respect, (when it's all you have); and there can be no doubt that, among her sister towns of Middlesex, Lowell must be considered as "large of her age."

With thanks for the kindness of the invitation, and assuring you of my sympathy with so pleasant an occasion.

I am very truly yours,

E. R. HOAR.

LETTER FROM HON. GEO. S. BOUTWELL.

UNITED STATES SENATE CHAMBER, WASHINGTON, Feb. 23, 1876.

To CHARLES COWLEY, ESQ., Lowell, Mass.

Sir,—At the time I received your invitation to attend the semi-centennial celebration of the incorporation of the town of Lowell, it appeared to me probable that I could be present. As the day approaches, I am compelled to abandon the thought, and I can only express to you my thanks for the honor of the invitation and my assurance that I rejoice with you in the many evidences of growth and prosperity which your city exhibits.

I am very truly, your most obedient servant,

GEO. S. BOUTWELL.

LETTER FROM COL. GEO. F. SAWTELL.

LYME, N. H., Feb. 28, 1876.

CHARLES COWLEY, ESQ., Chairman, &c., &c.

Dear Sir,—Your very kind invitation to attend the fiftieth anniversary of the incorporation of the town of Lowell was duly received.

I was in hopes to be present and enjoy the festivities of the occasion, but find myself at this late day unable to do so.

But having spent some thirty years of the best and happiest of my life in your goodly city, I can but feel a deep interest in your celebration. The warm grasp of the hand and the genial greeting that always receive me on visiting you, makes it a thrice happy place to me.

Although the wide world is open for my contemplation, the loved associations give a fascination to Lowell, that I find in no other place.

I am pleased to see that you have inaugurated a principle of moral suasion in regard to one of the greatest evils of the age, which is not confined to your city, but extends to the whole country; and if persevered in will do more to suppress the evil in two years than all the Courts and Legislation have done in the last twenty.

With your able Mayor at the head, backed by your many good citizens and a strong government, you will soon have little use for Courts and State Police.

Educate the people to do right; make a strong, healthy public opinion, and your future will be more glorious than the past, which has always been worthy of example.

Allow me to propose as a sentiment, The city of Lowell, with her roaring water-falls and the clatter of her many thousand looms; may they be but small in comparison to the joy of her fifty thousand happy sons and daughters.

Very respectfully, your obedient servant,

GEO. F. SAWTELL.

LETTER FROM GOV. ALEXANDER H. RICE.

COMMONWEALTH OF MASSACHUSETTS.
EXECUTIVE DEPARTMENT.
BOSTON, February 29, 1876.

CHARLES COWLEY, ESQ.

My Dear Sir,—I have your valued favor of the 25th inst., inviting me to attend the semi-centennial anniversary of the incorporation of the town of Lowell, on the first of March, and thank you for it.

It would afford me much pleasure to participate in ceremonies so interesting to yourself and your fellow-citizens, did not public duties require my presence here on that day.

I am, dear sir, with great respect,
Yours very truly,
ALEXANDER H. RICE.

LETTER FROM EX-GOVERNOR WASHBURN.

CAMBRIDGE, Feb. 28, 1876.

CHARLES COWLEY, ESQ., Chairman, &c.

Dear Sir,—I thank you for the honor of an invitation to be present at the commemoration of the fiftieth anniversary of the incorporation of the City of Lowell, and greatly regret that my duties here, on that day, will not permit me to enjoy the privilege of accepting it. But I cannot deny myself the pleasure of recalling, on such an occasion, the Lowell of thirty years ago, and the men I knew there in my brief residence in that city. It brings back the memories of the social and economical condition of a young, prosperous and thriving community, where honest labor was honored and intelligent skill and industry contributed, of their fruits, to the maintenance of schools and churches, while rearing and adorning pleasant and happy homes for themselves.

Lowell was, certainly, at that time, (and I will not say she has not always been), fortunate in the number of strong, able and public-spirited men, whose influence was felt in all the departments of business and social life. Coming, as its early citizens did from various localities in and beyond New England, the character, opinion and example of men like these had much to do not only in bringing these new elements of social life into harmony and consistancy, but in elevating and sustaining the tone and standard of public sentiment. It would be invidious to discriminate, and yet it would hardly be consistant with the purposes of such a letter to attempt to name them all. A few naturally occur to me now, from having been thrown into more especial intimacy by business relations with each other. And among them I would mention the names of Aiken, John Clark, Prince, the Wrights, John and Alexander, Bartlett and Child; to say nothing of the strong and able men whom they succeeded, among those connected with the manufacturing interests; French, Stickney, Dr. Huntington, Dr. Blanchard, Hopkinson and Wentworth, among the business and professional men, whose lives and services, if I might refer to them, would illustrate what I have said of the influence exerted by individual citizens upon the city itself. Obvious propriety has restricted me in thus speaking of the men of that day, to such as have already passed beyond the changes which may have since been wrought in the social fabric of the city; though I may, perhaps, be pardoned for referring to one whom I then new, though much my junior, who even then had given an earnest, within a narrower sphere, of qualities which have made his name familiar to the whole country, and who, I doubt not, will show himself, as he has so often done in the services and counsels of the nation, a *live man,* on the occasion of your proposed commemoration.

Permit me to add a single word of testimony in behalf of a city which has honored me by recognizing me as a former resident. When I knew Lowell better than I now do, she presented what has always seemed to me to be the best illustration and example that I have known, of what ought to be the true relation of labor and capital, in settling which so much wild speculation and fanciful theory have been expended. Instead of antagonism, real or fanciful oppression of the strong over the weak, there was a mutual regard for the interests of each. Capital furnished comfortable, convenient and respectable accomodations for the operatives, having regard to health, modes of living and facilities for labor, and contributed liberally in providing for the moral, educational and intellectual wants of these and their families. And they, on their part, being paid chiefly by piece work, were content to accept compensation in proportion to their skill and ability to earn it. They were, moreover, intelligent enough to know their own interests, and had self respect enough to command the consideration of their employers. Though employed, myself, to represent capital in its dealings with labor, I always found sympathy and aid on the part of the employees, in devising and carrying out a policy promotive of the best interests of both, without any occasion to call in the counsel of self created reformers, or to resort to a *strike* or a *lockout,* to force either to submit to the other. Lowell was then famed, the world over, for the intelligence of its operative classes, men and women, and my acquaintance with many of them confirmed, in my own mind, the justness of the estimate in which they were held.

You were pleased to ask me to say something " relating to matters of local interest," and, in attempting to do so, I fear I have transcended the proper limit of such a letter. But in looking back for the growth and character of your city for intelligence and good order on an occasion like that of commemorating its incorporation, it seemed to me that I owed to it a tribute of respect for its men and its institutions, as I had known them thirty years ago.

Very respectfully, your obedient servant,

EMORY WASHBURN.

LETTER FROM COL. THOMAS J. ADAMS.

NORTH CHELMSFORD, Feb. 28, 1876.

Gentlemen,—My recollections of Lowell date from many years before the building of your goodly city. My father, William Adams, was a soldier in the Revolutionary War, in the company of which the father of the late Franklin Pierce, President of the United States, was Captain; and among the incidents of that war which I have often heard him state during the long winter evenings, was the hanging of the gallant Major Andre, at Nyack, at which he was present. He kept the North Chelmsford Tavern forty years, ending April, 1840, with his death, at the age of eighty-two years.

The chairman of your committee has told me that he once heard a statement from Mrs. J. G. Abbott, daughter of Judge Livermore, and wife of Judge Abbott, that she had seen, in her girlhood, a thousand shad and one salmon caught at a single haul, near the mouth of the Concord River. The statement is no surprise to me. I have known three thousand six hundred shad to be caught by my father at Long Island, now in Lowell, in the space of twenty four hours. Fishing was only allowed on three days of each week.

In the second or third year after Mr. Boott came to Lowell, I sold him a fine salmon for which he paid me three five-dollar bills. It was used at a dinner of the Directors. It weighed twenty and one-half pounds, and was seventy-five cents per pound.

Captain Elisha Ford maintained as I do, that shad never go up the falls in the night, nor when the water is riley. Eels will.

Clark's Ferry was at Middlesex village. When General Varnum was buried under arms, in 1824, the Chelmsford Rifle Company did the honors, as they also did, afterwards, at the funeral of Capt. John Ford. Then it was, that the Pawtucket Bridge trembled and swung fearfully as the company marched over it keeping time. Our salute was three vollies. Capt. Ford told me the story of his killing an Indian in his saw-mill, as follows:

One day, Captain Ford went into his saw-mill at the foot of Pawtucket Falls, wearing his Revolutionary coat, bearing three brass buttons, each button being about two inches in diameter. He was not suspecting the presence of an enemy. He took up a bar to set a log to be sawed, when an Indian sprang upon him, shouting, "Me got you," and drawing a knife across his breast, over one of his big buttons. The button saved his life. Ford killed the Indian by a blow in the abdomen, which sent him out of the tail-race of the mill.

I was not aware till recently that this fact had ever been doubted. It was related more than once by Captain Ford in my hearing. Yours truly,

THOMAS. J. ADAMS.

LETTER FROM REV. HENRY E. HOVEY.

ST. BARNABAS RECTORY.
BROOKLYN, L. I., Feb. 29, 1876.

CHARLES COWLEY, ESQ., Chairman Committee of Arrangements.

Dear Sir,—I regret that an unavoidable claim for my presence in my parish on March first will prevent me from accepting your kind invitation to attend the semi-centennial of my native town.

It seems to me that there are three things which the sons whom Lowell has brought up and sent out into the world may be especially thankful to her for.

The first is a love for work. Perhaps more than any other of the large cities of this country Lowell is a municipality of labor. Thither there have gathered from far and near men of brain and men of muscle who have worked side by side for fifty years. The very air seems full of honest toil. They who have breathed it long should all have caught the inspiration, and if any son whom Lowell has reared and sent out has not been stimulated by these invigorating surroundings of his boyhood, it must be his own fault.

The second is a good education. More than usually generous is the provision which Lowell has made and does make for this. In common with all New England towns but in many respects foremost even among them, the schools have been well conducted by the authorities and well sustained by the people. Surely those of her sons who have gone out from her fostering care may be grateful to her for this.

The third is abundant religious training. A "cordon" of churches surrounding and protecting Lowell seem to lift themselves up in constant benediction upon her life. I believe that moral influences have a greater hold upon her people than in the average of American cities. Her sons ought to go forth strong and steadfast, taught to fear God and keep His commandments, trained to do their whole duty in that station of life unto which it hath pleased God to call them.

May there be a large gathering of the natives of Lowell at the semi-centennial coming up to bear testimony to their gratitude for these things; and may that fair and goodly town continue even to the remotest generation thus to bring up her children, that her children may always "rise up and call her blessed."

Very truly yours,
HENRY E. HOVEY.

LETTER FROM HON. FRANCIS B. CROWINSHIELD.

The Presidents, Treasurers, and past and present Resident Agents and Superintendents of all the Manufacturing Corporations of Lowell, were invited to the celebration, and many of them attended. Such of them as were unable so to do sent letters similar to this, from the veteran President of the Merrimack Manufacturing Company and of the Boston and Lowell Railroad.

BOSTON, Feb. 18, 1876.

CHARLES COWLEY, ESQ., Chairman, &c.

Dear Sir,—It would give me pleasure to avail myself of the kind invitation of the Committee of Arangements to attend the exercises on the first of March next, to commemorate the fiftieth anniversary of the incorporation of the Town of Lowell. But my engagements are such that it will not be in my power to do so.

I do not know of any matters of local interest to communicate, that are not well known to you and are not of general notoriety, although I was personally acquainted with the greater part of the men who first established the cotton manufacture in Lowell, and may therefore perhaps be justly called the founders of the town. With my thanks to yourself, and the gentlemen of the Committee, I am, truly yours,

F. B. CROWINSHIELD.

LETTER FROM MRS. CYRIL FRENCH.

LOWELL, Feb. 24, 1876.

CHARLES COWLEY, ESQ., Chairman.

Dear Sir,—To comply with the request of the committee, I will write something. I came to Lowell (East Chelmsford) the second day of December, 1824, and settled at the Swamp Locks, and have always taken a great interest in Lowell. It is barely possible that among my reminiscences I might be able to communicate something of interest. I can hardly realize that so many improvements could be made in fifty-one years.

When I came here, there were two cotton mills on the Merrimack, and Mr. Hurd's woollen mill at the Middlesex. There is not a mill in Lowell now, that was here then. Mr. Hurd's mill was burned in 1825, and one mill on the Merrimack was burned in January, 1829; the other was taken down to make room for larger ones.

There is a great contrast between *then* and *now*. Then there were no schools. A benevolent lady,* at the Swamp Locks, opened an "infant" school in her house; the children that could not keep awake were provided with beds. As is usual in the spring, the measles prevailed and the school was broken up for that season. The next year, there was a small school house built. Now look at the large and substantial buildings provided for our schools. Then we had no sidewalks; the mud was ankle deep in the spring. It was before rubber-shoes were brought from South America; if a pair of them could be seen now, they would be a great curiosity. And see the useful goods that are made from rubber.

And see the substantial concrete side-walks that hardly need rubber-shoes.

The first railway that was constructed in Lowell, was for the purpose of conveying in carts the earth that was taken out of the so-called "new canal" (now the western) to make land for the Carpet Mills. We had one nice house in our neighborhood, built on Worthen Street in 1823 and 1824, for Mr. Paul Moody, the agent for the Machine Shop. It had a beautiful lawn in front, sloped down to a handsome pond on Dutton Street, which was spoiled soon after he died, by being filled up and covered with ten-foot buildings, the only place that has not been improved in looks. The building still stands there, but none of its beauty. Then we had candles and sperm oil to burn; two can-

*Mrs. Nathan Oliver.

dles or a lamp with two wicks made an extra light. Now look at the gas-jets everywhere.

I have a distinct recollection of those who came here from Waltham: Paul Moody Nathan Oliver, Samuel Oliver, Joshua Swan, A. W. Fisher, Samuel S. Fisher, William Mason, George Brownell, William Walker, Samuel Walker, Capt. James Derby, Isaac Anthony, Mr. Webster, Mr. Gates, and their several families.

I shall be most happy to be present at the exercises on Wednesday afternoon, and am very much obliged for the invitation.

Respectfully yours,

MRS. CYRIL FRENCH.

LETTER FROM EX-GOV. E. A. STRAW.

MANCHESTER, N. H., Feb. 22, 1876.

CHARLES COWLEY, ESQ., Chairman, Lowell, Mass.

Dear Sir,—I have to acknowledge the receipt of yours of February 5th, kindly inviting me to "attend the exercises for commemorating, on the first of March next, the fiftieth anniversary of the incorporation of the town of Lowell." I shall certainly endeavor to be present.

A resident of the town, forty years ago, for ten years of my boyhood and youth, my recollections of early companions and knowledge of later friends are all of the most agreeable character, and such as will make a celebration of the kind you propose very attractive to me.

Yours very truly,

E. A. STRAW.

LETTER FROM SAMUEL WEBBER.

MANCHESTER, N. H., Feb. 23, 1876.

CHARLES COWLEY, ESQ., Chairman, &c.

Dear Sir,—It will afford me great pleasure to accept your invitation of the 5th inst., and attend the semi-centennial celebration of Lowell on the first of March.

I have many pleasant recollections of the city where I served my apprenticeship in mechanics and manufactures. Though it has changed much from the days when I used to sit in Nathaniel Wright's office in the Wyman building, and take an evening smoke, looking out over a lumber yard, and a vast stretch of pasture land, now occupied, respectively, by the Prescott Mills, and the pleasant residences of Belvidere.

Many a Saturday afternoon have I spent botanizing with the late John D. Prince in "Osgood's woods," and the valley below the Powder Mills, where wild flowers must be few and far between now.

The Merrimack Company at my first acquaintance with it had six printing machines and the Hamilton Company three, and soon after I came to Lowell Mr. Boyden put in the first turbine wheel, and the Locks and Canals Company made the first measurements of water in the Merrimack Canals.

Manufacturing was hardly reduced to a science then, and I have no doubt that some of your citizens will remember when the late Robert Means looked in vain for the overseers in one of the Suffolk Mills, one afternoon, till he found them all in the attic, rolling nine-pins, with Speeder Bobbins and Balls of "Thrums."

The City Library, the Commons, and the Cemetery, have all been matters of growth within my recollection, and there are many other remembrances, which I can recall but which are hardly worth putting on record.

With many thanks for the kind recollection implied by the invitation, I remain, yours very sincerely,

SAMUEL WEBBER.

LETTER FROM REV. EDWARD COWLEY.

157 EAST 60TH STREET.
NEW YORK, Feb. 22, 1876.

Gentlemen,—It will afford me great pleasure to attend your semi-centennial celebration, if in my power to be present.

I observe that the distinguished orator* who preached the historical sermon at the recent celebration of your First Baptist Church, dwelt very tenderly and lovingly on the extraordinary ministry of the lamented E. W. Freeman. "Its beginning was a song; its end a tragedy," he says; and such indeed it was; nor have there been wanting many intelligent persons who have ever since believed that his own wife was guilty of "the deep damnation of his taking off."

It having fallen to my lot to be the clergyman to whom "that wicked woman" (as Dr. Eddy calls Mr. Freeman's widow) applied for

---
* Rev. Daniel C. Eddy, D. D. This sermon has been printed.

spiritual counsel as her end drew near, I may be pardoned for communicating a few facts relating to her death.

More than once during her last sickness she told me that she had something that she wished to communicate to me in relation to her own life, but she put it off from time to time. She died during my absence from the city, and the secrets of her life, whatever they were, went to the grave with her. She was buried in God's Acre, the Protestant division of the cemetery at Ward's Island, from which the bodies have since been removed to Hart's Island, so that her grave is entirely unknown and unknowable. Copying from the official records at the Almshouse I find that "Hannah Freeman, native of Maine, for twenty-five years of the city and county of New York, died of Bright's disease, on the 28th of June 1868, and was buried in the Protestant section of the city cemetery." It was a most sad termination of a career once of great promise.

Yours truly,

EDWARD COWLEY.

LETTER FROM HON. PETER LAWSON.

LOWELL, Feb. 29, 1876.

Gentlemen,—I accept with pleasure your invitation of the 25th inst., and as I am the only man now living of those who came from Medway to Lowell in 1829, I will give you my recollections of that "Medway Colony." The manufacture of ingrain carpets was started in Medway in 1826, by Alexander Wright and Eben Burditt of Boston. They had ten ingrain looms, one Brussells loom, and one finger-rugg loom, and their establishment was the first of the kind in the United States. They were in successful operation in 1827, when a committee consisting of Frederick Cabot, George W. Lyman and Patrick T. Jackson, visited their establishment, bought out all they had and took them into their own employ.

The Lowell Manufacturing Company, organized in 1828, ordered them to build fifty more ingrain looms, eleven more Brussells looms and seven more finger-rugg looms. All who had been employed in the carpet manufacture in Medway, (except Mr. Burditt,) removed in 1829 to Lowell. They were Alexander Wright, Agent; Peter Lawson, pattern designer; Claudius Wilson, foreman; Royal Southwick, overseer; John Urie, section hand on looms; Joseph Exley, overseer Brussells loom; John Robertson, overseer dye house; John Hughes, overseer dye house; Daniel Thurston, second overseer dye house; John

Turnbull, carpet cloth room; David Wilson,* dyer; Henry Chandler, wood workman; Benjamin Smith, wood workman; George W. Hunt, wood workman; William Wilson, finger-rugg weaver; Samuel Townsend, Thomas Railton, Job Plimpton, Gilmore Pond, Abel Brummett, Otis Bemis, Albert Adams, Hector McArthur and Benjamin Albee, weavers.

Frederick Cabot was the first Treasurer and Frederick Emmerson the first Clerk. Mr. Wright, the leader of the Medway Colony, remained agent of the Lowell Company till his death, June 8, 1852, at the age of fifty-two. His widow still survives, and resides in this city, as does also Mrs. William Wilson. Mr. Southwick's widow also survives, in Boston. The inventions of Claudius Wilson were fully described in the Glasgow Magazine for 1826. He was one of the most ingenious mechanics whom Scotland has contributed to aid in the development of the mechanic arts.

The brick buildings of the company were erected by Elijah M Reed, who came to Lowell from Waltham, and who had charge of all building operations under the late Mr. Sanger.

The first railroad I ever saw, and probably the first in America, extended from the Suffolk Canal through the wood of Lowell Street, (then a dense forest), to the Lowell Company's grounds. The cars were drawn by horses, under Hugh Cummiskey, contractor, who, with the excavations of the Suffolk Canal, made the land where the Carpet Company's Mills now stand, much of it being twenty feet deep.

One thing that surprises me, was the novel manner of constructing the foundations. These were laid on the original surface and the earth filled in around them to the desired height. Wells were constructed in the same way, the stone curbing being laid on the top of the old ground, and new ground made around it till a well of the desired depth had been *built up*. The first building erected by the Carpet Company was the one and a half story block now standing, near the counting room. There for some time were my own quarters, and many a string of fine pickerel have I caught sitting on the front steps, from the branch canal (built in the same way as the wells), the waters of which washed the steps of my door. In later years, when the canal was constructed to the width originally designed, the present street was constructed between the block and the canal. These peculiarities arose from the fact that the land selected for the Carpet Company was originally a low swamp. Yours truly,

PETER LAWSON.

* He was a younger brother of Alexander Wilson, the celebrated ornithologist.

LETTER FROM JOHN F. McEVOY.

LOWELL, Feb. 22, 1876.

CHARLES COWLEY, ESQ.

My dear Sir,—I thank you for your invitation to the Semi-Centennial Celebration of the birth of our city, and regret that a business engagement will prevent my presence, but I can not allow the occasion to pass without bearing my testimony to the enterprise and labor expended by yourself, and others in our midst, to perpetuate the ancient history of our town, before it is forgetten. It is always pleasant for me to recur to the more ancient days when Lowell was a series of farms, when Charles Street was a cranberry-meadow, and when a farmer's little daughter, now a venerable matron, drove the cows to water at the spring where now John Street pump is located. Still later, when one could go across lots from Central Street to the Town House, by cutting through a foot path in the swampy ground now occupied by Middle Street and the surrounding territory. You do a great public good, in my opinion, in keeping alive our ancient history, and if it were a possible thing I should like to aid you, although no better way occurs to me than to send a few data I have been able to gather concerning the early Irish settlers in the city.

The pioneer among these was Mr. Hugh Cummiskey, who came here with thirty men from Charlestown, all on foot, to work on the canals. Kirk Booot met them at what is now the American House, gave them money to refresh themselves, and they went right to work widening the old Pawtucket Canal and building the new ones. Ground was first broken, in this kind of work, on the 6th of April, 1822. From this time forward, the town became the centre of attraction for the hard working Irish laborer, many of whom afterwards settled here, became most reputable citizens, and some few left families behind them to perpetuate their name and fame. The town was then in a most primitive condition and the laboring classes contented themselves with the rudest kind of habitation. In 1828, they had mostly concentrated themselves in that part of the town lying west of the Suffolk Canal and north of Broadway, still known as the "Acre." It is somewhat difficult at this time to conceive, that then with the exception of a few houses in the woods, back of the First Congregational Meeting House, (Dr. Blanchard's), it was all an open common between the American House and Pawtucket Falls, but such was the fact, and it was upon this ground that the laborers pitched their camps, their tents, or whatever was attainable to shelter their hardy natures from the wind and rain. The title to some of this land was afterwards called in question and it was eventually decided by the United States Supreme Court in Washington under the name of the "Paddy Camp Lands" and the case is known in the books, to this day, by that title.

It may not be unknown to you that the history of the Irish is almost identical with that of their Church. Their efforts outside of the attainment of creature comforts, have invariably spent themselves in developing their religion and furnishing means and facilities for its enjoyment. The Bishop of the Diocese came among them in person Oct. 28, 1828, and religious services were held in a two-story school house next above Dr. Blanchard's meeting house on Merrimack Street, which was owned by the town and loaned to the three or four hundred catholics, then here, for the purposes of religious worship. Father John Mahoney after that used to come regularly once a month from Salem to celebrate Mass, and regularly the children were taught the Catechism, and a day school was established, in which the ordinary English branches were taught by a schoolmaster who previously had found the same employment in Ireland. This was one of the pioneer schools of Lowell. Prominent among the Irishmen of these times were Hugh Cummiskey, Patrick McManus, his Superintendent, Nicholas Fitzpatrick, Patrick Powers, grocer, Edward Kitts, shoemaker, and John Green who was a gardener by trade and was Mr. Boott's steward.

The Irish grew apace in number and the little school house grew too small for their needs. Kirk Boott, representing the Locks and Canals Corporation, gave the Bishop the land on Fenwick Street, where now St Patrick's Church stands, and a frame building seventy by forty feet was projected in the month of July, 1830, and such was the harmony and united zeal developed in the enterprise that it was dedicated in twelve months from that time, much to the chagrin unfortunately of some disfavored few who were unwilling to see a Catholic Church erected in the town. Bishop Fenwick and Rev. Dr. O'Flaherty came from Boston the day before in a carryall, and took lodgings at the Stone House now the residence cf Dr. J. C. Ayer. The church was dedicated under the auspices of St. Patrick, July 3, 1831, and Dr. O'Flaherty delivered the dedication sermon preaching from the text " This place I have chosen as a house of sacrifice and prayer."

The music at the dedication of the church was furnished by the Cathedral choir of Boston, assisted by Mr. Edward Kitts, Mr. Hector and Miss Catherine Hogan of Lowell.

The old church as I have said was a frame building, seventy by forty feet, and was of course small, but sufficient to accommodate the Irish catholics in the town. In 1832, Father Mahoney built the priest's house, which was located next the church, and, having within a few years been moved away, is now located on Lewis, directly opposite Fenwick Street.

In 1835, Rev. Father Curtin came to Lowell as assistant priest to Rev. Father Mahoney, and staid here only a short time, being displaced by Rev. Father Connelly, who, under Father Mahoney's direction and with his assistance, built the two wings to the church, making it cruciform in shape and exactly in the form in which it existed many years and was afterwards dismantled and taken down.

Many of those, who will read this, cannot fail to remember Rev. Father J. T. McDermott who succeeded Rev. Father Mahoney in the spiritual care of the Irish Catholics of Lowell in the summer of 1837. His memory is fresh in the minds of many of our citizens. Father Mahoney removed to New Bedford and died there, in the active ministration of the Gospel.

In 1839, Rev. James Conway was appointed Father McDermott's assistant, and was not here long before the necessity for a new church became apparent to him, which was made more necessary from the fact that the Irish were settling in around William, Green, and Gorham Streets and were consequently too far away from the old church on Fenwick Street to make their religious duties easy to them.

He secured the lot on the corner of Gorham and Appleton Streets in August 1841, upon which he built the brick church still standing but much enlarged, which was dedicated, under the auspices of St. Peter, Oct. 16, 1842.

Prominent among the Irish Catholics in this time were Mr. Hugh McEvoy, tailor, still living, John Quinn, tailor, also still living, Mr. Edward Connelly, Mr. Owen M. Donohoe, who kept the Exchange Coffee House on Lowell Street, Mr. Charles M. Short, Mr. Peter McDermott, a brother of the clergyman, Mr. Patrick Moran, dry goods dealer, Nicholas Ryan, dealer in crockery, Michael McDonough, dealer in dry goods, and Maguire & Cassidy, also very enterprising dealers in dry goods, John O'Conner and Michael Cassidy.

The Old Fifth Grammer School, now the Mann School, was then a very important item in the social life of the Irish Catholics of the town. Mr. James Egan, afterwards a prominent lawyer in Boston, was the first Irish Catholic principal of the school, assisted by Mr. Peter McDermott and Miss Esther Howland. It was the school where most of the now middle-aged Irish Catholics of the town received their Grammar School education. Mr. Daniel McElroy was also a teacher in this school, who subsequently achieved quite a reputation as a lawyer in Chicago, Ill., where he died a few years ago.

I ought not to fail to mention the name of Mr. Cornelius Nolan, who came to Lowell and resided here in 1844-5-6, superintending the erection of a portion of the famous new canal, which changed the whole method of taking the water from our river, for manufacturing purposes.

The more recent Irish Catholic history of the town is so familiar that I need not take up your attention by adverting to it, but lest the dates connected with it may not hereafter be accessible, I may be permitted to refer to them.

Rev. Father Conway was removed to Salem in March, 1847, and Rev. Peter Crudden installed in his place as his successor. Rev. Father McDermott purchased St. Mary's Church on Suffolk Street, of the Baptists, and it was dedicated in 1847, and after the brief pastorate of Rev. Father Tucker, the Rev. Fathers Timothy and John O'Brien were appointed to the pastorate of old St Patrick's. The magnificent new church now erected on the site of the old frame building by these zealous clergymen, was dedicated in October, 1854.

The Academy of Notre Dame on Adams Street, in the care of the Sisters of Notre Dame, now so flourishing, which gives constant employment to nearly thirty teachers, and which maintains a free school for over six hundred and fifty pupils, with a boarding school for nearly one hundred and forty, was established in 1853.

St Peter's School and Orphan Asylum under the charge of the Sisters of Charity, a refuge for over seventy orphans, was established in 1866.

St. John's Hospital, under the same charge, which can accomodate nearly seventy patients, was incorporated by special act of the Legislature in 1867.

All these institutions have ever since their establishment been prosecuting their useful work quietly and in the face of many difficulties, but in such a manner as to make their final success assured.

As if the Irish Catholics in the town and city of Lowell had not done all that was needed to secure their permanent comfort and maintain their personal needs, the magnificent stone church, now in process of erection in Belvidere, will be before another year dedicated to the services of religion. The society of Oblates for poor missions have this in charge, as also a mission church for the French Catholics, who are already numerous enough to fill the church in Lee

Street, which they purchased from the Unitarian denomination some years ago, and have increased its size to double its former capacity.

I do not desire to intrude further upon your time or upon the space you may possibly wish to give this communication.

The data I am aware are extremely meagre, but they will be sufficient to give those who live after us, some general idea of the part the Irish Catholics have taken in the early history of the town and city. Very truly yours,

JOHN F. McEVOY.

LEVEE.

The Semi-Centennial Levee was attended by a great concourse of the past and present residents of Lowell. The settees having been removed, a fine opportunity was afforded for promenading, and the exchange of friendly greetings, while the Germania Band discoursed enlivening music. No speeches were called for; but Mr. Ordway, of Newton, read the following poem:

POEM.
By John L. Ordway.

In all the ages gone, in every clime,
Men have dwelt fondly on the olden time,
Investing it, as, through the golden haze,
Its mellowed glories rose to memory's gaze,
With splendors brilliant, hues of living light,
And peopling every hillside, plain and glen,
With nobler races, heroes, God-like men,
Appearing grander as they passed from sight.
The present, glowing with its noon-day blaze,
Is dimmed and darkened by the brighter rays
That stream upon us from the "Light of other
    days."

'Tis well, sometimes, to pause upon life's track,
And, through the distance, cast our glances back,
Contrast the progress of this age so fast,
With the slow movements of the misty past,
Imbibe fresh wisdom from the days long fled,
And then march onward with a firmer tread.

And now when the centennial year
With every thronging memory is here,
Our thoughts go back and dwell upon that time,

Of noble men and deeds sublime;
The days of hardship and of trial,
Of sore distress, heroic self-denial,
Of suffering unto death, all that the land,
Freed from the iron grasp of tyrant hand,
Forevermore might be
The dwelling place of liberty.
Then lived the men whose labors and whose zeal
Were less for private ends than public weal;
Whose virtues—an enduring heritage—
Shall be revered by each successive age,
And, as along time's rapid stream shall flow,
Shall still with fresher, brighter colors glow.
But here and now we linger not to trace
The scenes and trials of those older days;
These swelling hearts, these tearful eyes
Are moved not by a nation's destinies;
These thoughts of mingled joy and pain,
Of sunshine now, and now of rain,
Are marked by other dear remembrances,
For turning o'er time's record, there appears
Upon the pages marking "Fifty years,"
In short and simple language noted down
The annals of a Town.
No deeds of high emprise,
Of great renown,
Were done the day to signalize
When, mid the roar of waterfalls,
The plunge and rush through rocky walls
As swept the noble river by
In all its strength and majesty,
And earth was fair, and skies were bright to see,
Armed and equipped, and ready for the fray
Lowell—Minerva like—first saw the light of day.
Old honored Chelmsford, weary years and long,
Had heard the cadence of the river's song,
Its ceaseless roar of sad monotony
As it rolled onward to the distant sea.
At length, awaking from a sleep profound,
With strength renewed she rose, surveyed the
    ground,

And said, with kindling eye and eager haste,
"This water shall no longer run to waste."
And soon the clatter of machinery,
The hum of busy industry,
The promise of the great "To be"
Were heard from yonder factory.
And, when the stranger from the city came,
She gave her first and only child his name.
And now young Lowell waves abroad his hand,
Mills, workshops, dwellings rise at his command.
He sends his summons forth, and lo! from far
   and near
Men, women, children at his call appear;
From distant lands beyond the Ocean wide
See thousands rushing to his side!

Vain the attempt to tell in prose, or rhyme,
Of all the changes since the early time
Transcending all the marvels brought
From fancy's realm of busy thought,
Imagination's highest flight,
Fair visions of poetic sight,
Wild fables of mythology,
The queer conceits of legends told
Around the "blazing hearths" of old,
And every curious fantasy
Fleeting, ephemeral, of what might be
E'en our historian's graceful pen would fail,
If not "to point the moral," "to adorn the tale."
What is to-day, we all can plainly see,
What whilom was, is known imperfectly.
Go learn the history from those
Whose heads are whitened like the winter's
   snows.
Few, few alas! from those old days remain:
But talking of the "Good old times" they're
   young again,
And pleasant 'tis to see their faces glow
As they rehearse the scenes of long-ago,
When Worthen came from distant Amesbury,
(Where still doth "winding Powow fold
The green hill in its belt of gold")

To "spy the land" with Moody, and to see
What promise for the future there might be;
When Jackson, Lowell, Boott and Appleton
Said "This shall be," and it was done;
And factories with clattering din and roar
Usurped the scene of peaceful joys of yore,
When Colburn lived across the street near by;
(Ah! how his problems our poor brains did try:)
And when New England's glory and its pride—
Churches and free schools side by side
Were, in that school-house, first established
    here:
Man's wisdom teaching through the long six
    days,
But on the seventh, precious truths and dear,
And rendering to the Source of all glad praise.

But hark! from yonder tower we hear the chimes;
They ring the melodies of olden times.
That sacred church has half a century stood,
Still may it stand through tempest and through
    flood,
A noble monument of good—
Till countless ages shall have passed.
It was the first; so may it be the last.

And now one venerable form appears—
Surviving through the swiftly flying years.
Untiring, active as in days gone by
In Christ-like deeds of heavenly charity,
Relieving want, and speaking words of cheer,
Making life brighter, bringing Heaven more near,
From early morn to set of sun
Seeking some duty to be done,
Teaching by daily life and walk
Far better than by wordy talk
"The Luxury of doing good"
That needs no recompense of gratitude,
He points, he guides unto the better way
Which leads unto the "perfect day."

Some things there are belonging to the past
That we would have forever last.

Some that are gone we sigh for now in vain,
And memory, only, brings them back again.

Give us the old once more!
Speak voice of other days!
Those homely joys restore.
On bright scenes let us gaze
That, in the earlier time
When we were in our prime,
Met our enraptured vision
And seemed like Fields Elysian.

Give us old friends again!
How memory recalls
The walks through glade and glen
And by the river's falls!
And pleasant 'twas to greet,
Whene'er we chanced to meet,
The true and noble hearted
Who have from earth departed.

Give us to keep for aye
Those old friends true and tried
Who live, and stand to-day
As firmly by our side
As in the days gone by—
When life flowed peacefully—
Ere grief and care so carking,
Our brows with lines were marking.

Let the old songs be sung—
The Sabbath evening hymn
That rose from old and young
Amid the twilight dim.
No strains the heart can move
Like those sweet tones we love—
Dear precious memories bringing
Of angel voices singing.

The good that was of yore,
Long may its influence last!
The evil, known no more,
Is numbered with the past.
Those early pioneers,

Still bright each name appears,
Each filling well his station
In his day and generation.

Lowell ! still may each son
Thee in his heart enshrine,
And, till life's day is done,
Remember thee and thine.
May thy prosperity
Greater and better be
As, like yon swiftly flowing river,
The years roll on—and on—forever.

FIRST FRUITS OF THE CELEBRATION.

HAPGOOD WRIGHT CENTENNIAL TRUST FUND.

The following letter illustrates the sentiments which the Semi-Centennial Celebration tended to diffuse.

LOWELL, March 7, 1876.

To the City Council of the City of Lowell:

Gentlemen,—Having lived in the town and city of Lowell since 1828, and been in trade since 1830, and I believe now the only person in Lowell in trade at that date, and being thankful to Almighty God for his great goodness to me, I therefore wish in this form to give unto others of my fellow-men, for their benefit and improvement in the future here in Lowell, where I have lived so long and enjoyed so much, the small gift of one thousand dollars, if the City Council will accept the same upon the following conditions, to wit: I wish the money to be put on interest for fifty years, the centennial year of the town of Lowell, and the interest added to the principal, either annually or semi-annually, until that time, when all but the original sum of one thousand dollars may be expended for the benefit and improvement of the city or citizens of Lowell as the City Council may determine, by a two-thirds vote of said City Council, in joint convention assembled, and if the City Council should not be able to command a two-thirds vote upon the manner of disposing of the same at that time, it may be left to succeeding city governments to dispose of by the same two-thirds vote of the City Council. The original one thousand dollars shall again be put at interest as before described, and at the end of every fifty years thereafter, all but the original principal may be disposed of in the same manner as before mentioned.

Respectfully yours,

HAPGOOD WRIGHT.

N. B.—If there is no objection it may be called the Hapgood Wright Centennial Trust Fund. H. W.

This letter was read in both branches of the City Council, on March 14th. In the Board of Aldermen, Alderman Goodwin offered the following resolution:

RESOLVED, By the Board of Aldermen, and Common Council of the City of Lowell, in City Council assembled as follows:

That the donation offered by Hapgood Wright of One Thousand Dollars, be accepted; that the Fund thereby created be called the Hapgood Wright Centennial Trust Fund; and that the City Council, approving the purposes expressed in the letter of donation, do agree, in behalf of the City, to execute the trust proposed therein, in conformity with the conditions therein expressed.

In the Common Council, Councilman Charles Cowley spoke as follows:

REMARKS OF COUNCILMAN COWLEY ON THE WRIGHT TRUST FUND.

I am sure, Mr. President, that no argument is needed to induce the City Council to accept the trust which this public spirited citizen offers to create; but I wish to express my gratification with this donation, considering it as only one of the first fruits of the recent public commemoration of the fiftieth anniversary of our municipal nativity, which I had the honor to initiate more than a year ago. Mr. Wright, whose letter is now before us, was then a member of the Board of Aldermen, and was also a member of the Committee which made all the arrangements for that celebration. He took a warm interest in it from the start, and he now further signalizes the event by the creation of this noble trust. It cannot be inopportune, while this letter is before us, to glance at the career of the gentleman whose name is now to be forever enrolled among the benefactors of our city.

Hapgood Wright was born in Concord in 1811, and graduated at the public schools of that ancient town. In 1828, at the age of seventeen, he came to Lowell, and two years later, while still a minor, he started in the boot and shoe business, on the spot where the Boston and Andover Railroad depot now stands. After several previous changes of location, in 1840 he located himself at No. 51 Central Street, where he still remains. He is the oldest living merchant now in business in Lowell, and has never changed his business; but, faithful to the *ne-suitor* maxim, has "steadily stuck to his last," and demonstrated that, "try what you will, there is nothing like leather." Through all the vicissitudes of nearly half a century, he has never suspended payment, but ploughed right through all periods of panic and depression, 1837, 1857, and also 1873, 1874, and 1875, when even the Merrimack Manufacturing Company passed its dividend.

He has always enjoyed the fullest confidence of his fellow-citizens. He served two years in this branch, and four years in the other branch of the City Council, and two years in the General Court. He has been connected with two of our Banks of Discount—the Lowell and the Prescott—and a Trustee of the Five Cent Savings Bank ever since its incorporation in 1854, and is Chairman of its Board of Investments. He was one of the founders of the Ministry at Large, and has been a constant and liberal contributor to its funds. The services which Mr. Wright has rendered, of which I have mentioned only the more conspicuous, and by no means the most important, have been rendered *gratis*. Except for his services in the General Court, he has never received a dollar for anything done in any public capacity; and, what is not to be forgotten by any one in this country, he has always borne in mind the fact that our government is a government of all, and by all, and for all, and not merely of those, or by those, or for those, whom the chance-medley of an election or the caprices of cliques or coteries may place in public positions at any given time.

Since reading this letter of Mr. Wright, I have been trying to recall the names of other Lowell people who have heretofore contributed of their means to public objects. I recall Mary Barnard, who left sixty dollars to Oberlin College; James G. Carney, whose contribution of one hundred dollars has provided those Carney Medals, for which the boys and girls of our High School annually compete; James C. Ayer, who gave Lowell the statue of "Victory" which ornaments an adjoining square; Abner W. Buttrick, who gave ten thousand dollars to Harvard University, and Tappan Wentworth, for many years the neighbor and bosom friend of Mr. Wright, whose princely bequest to Darmouth College will perpetuate his name with honor as long as our present form of civilization endures. Mr. Wentworth also gave one thousand dollars to the Old Ladies' Home, and a part of his law library for the use of the local Bar.

To this list I might add those who gave with a liberal hand to the cause of the Union during the Civil War, and those who have made donations for denominational purposes. These I omit; but there are two others who must not be omitted—Thomas Nesmith, whose gift of twenty-five thousand dollars created the Nesmith Fund for the

Poor, and Henry F. Durant, the founder of Wellesley College for Women. If some of these have made larger gifts, none, I am sure, have given from worthier motives than the founder of the Hapgood Wright Centennial Trust Fund; and I can express no better hope for our city than that in the long aftertime she may always have citizens as worthy of her confidence, esteem and pride as the founder of this Fund.

CITY OFFICERS.

The officers of the city of Lowell for the year 1876, being the Semi Centennial year of our Municipality and the Centennial year of our Republic, are as follows:

MAYOR:

CHARLES A. STOTT.

ALDERMEN:

Chairman—JOHN A. GOODWIN.

JACOB ROGERS,	HENRY A. HILDRETH,
JOHN A. GOODWIN,	GEORGE E. STANLEY,
ALBERT A. HAGGETT,	FRANCIS CARLL,
CHARLES F. BELDEN,	WILLIAM H. WIGGIN.

COMMON COUNCIL:

President—JOHN F. KIMBALL.*

Ward One.

JOHN W. WELCH,	DANIEL W. MANNING,
LEWIS STILES,	JOHN F. HOWARD.†

Ward Two.

LEAVITT R. J. VARNUM,	CHARLES CALLAHAN,
CHARLES E. HALLOWELL,	WILLIAM A. READ.

Ward Three.

CHARLES COWLEY,	CHARLES RUNELS,
CHARLES H. KIMBALL,	WILLIAM H. GRADY.‡

*Elected May 23rd, on the resignation of Benjamin C. Dean.
†Elected January 11th, in place of David M. Collins, who declined to serve.
‡ Elected January 11th, in place of James Howard, who died before his term began.

OFFICERS OF THE CITY GOVERNMENT.

Ward Four.

GARDNER W. KING,
STEPHEN H. JONES,

CHARLES D. STARBIRD,
JAMES W. BENNETT.¶

Ward Five.

ORFORD R. BLOOD,
JOHN F. KIMBALL,

CHARLES H. HANSON,
M. GILBERT PERKINS.

Ward Six.

EDWIN SANBORN,
CHARLES H. WALKER,

JOHN J. PICKMAN,
WILLIS FARRINGTON.§

CITY CLERK:
SAMUEL A. MCPHETRES.

MESSENGER TO THE CITY COUNCIL:
JOHN H. NICHOLS.

CITY TREASURER AND COLLECTOR OF TAXES:
JOHN H. MCALVIN.

CLERK OF THE COMMON COUNCIL AND AUDITOR OF ACCOUNTS:
DAVID CHASE.

SUPERINTENDENT OF STREETS:
JOHN C. WOODWARD.

CIVIL ENGINEER FOR THE CITY:
GEORGE E. EVANS.

CITY SOLICITOR:
GEORGE F. RICHARDSON.

¶Elected June 22nd, in place of Edward Stockman, who resigned.
§ Elected June 22nd, in place of Benjamin C. Dean, who resigned.

DIRECTORS OF THE CITY LIBRARY:

CHARLES A. STOTT, Mayor,
JOHN F. KIMBALL, President of the Common Council. } *Ex-Officiis.*

Ward 1—CHARLES H. HARVEY,   Ward 4—ABNER A. JEWETT,
" 2—FRANK E. RICE,   " 5—GEORGE SMITH,
" 3—CHARLES F. TILTON,   " 6—JAMES C. ABBOTT.

LIBRARIAN OF THE CITY LIBRARY:
MARSHALL H. CLOUGH.

SUPERINTENDENT OF PUBLIC BUILDINGS:
LORENZO G. HOWE.

CITY PHYSICIAN AND SUPERINTENDENT OF BURIALS:
HERMON J. SMITH.

ASSESSORS OF TAXES:

FRANCIS GOWARD,   ISAAC A. FLETCHER,
JAMES MARREN,   LEVI B. STEVENS,
WILLIAM W. READ,   DAVID LANE.
FRANCIS GOWARD, *Chairman.* JAMES MARREN, *Secretary.*

OVERSEERS OF THE POOR:

CHARLES A. STOTT,   JOHN F. MCEVOY,
NATHANIEL C. SANBORN,   JOSIAH BUTLER
CHARLES COWLEY,   SULLIVAN L. WARD.
LEAVITT R. J. VARNUM,   FREDERICK HOLTON, Secretary.

SUPERINTENDENT OF THE INSTITUTIONS AT THE CITY FARM:
LORENZO PHELPS.

Matron—MRS. SARAH PHELPS.

Chaplain and Teacher—WILLIAM A. LANG.

LOWELL WATER BOARD:

President—CYRUS H. LATHAM.

From the City Council.—Alderman ALBERT A. HAGGETT, Councilmen JOHN F. KIMBALL and ORFORD R. BLOOD.

OFFICERS OF THE CITY GOVERNMENT.

From the Citizens at Large.—CYRUS H. LATHAM.

Superintendent—SAMUEL P. GRIFFIN.

CITY MARSHAL:
WILLIAM H. CLEMENCE.

DEPUTY MARSHALL:
JACOB G. FAVOR.

CHIEF ENGINEER:
GEORGE HOBSON.

ASSISTANT ENGINEERS:
SAMUEL W. TAYLOR,   EDWARD S. HOSMER,
HIRAM N. HALL, Clerk of the Board.

SCHOOL COMMITTEE:
Chairman—CHARLES A. STOTT.
Vice Chairman—EPHRAIM B. PATCH.
Secretary—CHARLES MORRILL.

CHARLES A STOTT, Mayor. } *Ex-Officiis.*
JOHN F. KIMBALL, President of the Common Council. }

WILLIAM M. HOAR,	HENRY P. CARTER,
JAMES W. B. SHAW,	CHARLES KIMBALL,
ROBERT L. READ,	JOHN J. COLTON,
GEORGE H. PILLSBURY,	WILLIAM G. WARD,
JOHN J. GREEN,	LORENZO S. FOX,
EPHRAIM B. PATCH,	GEORGE F. LAWTON.

POLICE COURT OF LOWELL:
Standing Justice—NATHAN CROSBY.
Special Justices { —JOHN DAVIS,
                 { —FREDERICK T. GREENHALGE.
Clerk—SAMUEL P. HADLEY.

SELECTMEN OF LOWELL DURING THE TOWN ORGANIZATION, 1826 - 1836.

Batchelder, Samuel, 1826.
Chase, John, 1835–36.
Coburn, Henry, Jr., 1827.
Crosby, Josiah, 1832.
Fox, Jesse, 1834.
Huntington, Elisha, 1833–34.
Livingston, William, 1834–35–36.
Oliver, Samuel C., 1832–33.
Owen. William N., 1835–36.
Parkhurst, Matthias, 1832–33.

Russell, James, 1835–36.
Swan, Joshua, 1827–28–29–30–31–32–33–34.
Tyler, James, 1830–31.
Walker, Benjamin, 1832–33–34–35–36.
Whipple, Oliver M., 1826.
Wright, Nathaniel, 1826–27–28–29.
Young, Artemas, 1828–29–30–31.

MAYORS AND MEMBERS OF THE CITY COUNCIL, 1836 - 1876.

MAYORS.

Ayer, James H. B., 51.
Bancroft, Jefferson, 46, 47, 48.
Bartlett, Elisha, 36, 37.
Cook, James, 59.
Folsom, Jonathan P., 69, 70.
French, Josiah B., 49, 50.
Hosford, Hocum, 62, 63, 64.
Huntington, Elisha, 39, 40, 41, 44, 45, 52, 56, 58.
Jewett, Francis, 73, 74, 75.

Lawrence, Ambrose, 55.
Lawrence, Luther, 38, 39.
Mack, Sewall G., 53, 54.
Mansur, Stephen, 57.
Peabody, Josiah G., 65, 66, 72.
Richardson, George F., 67, 68.
Sargeant, Benjamin C., 60, 61.
Sherman, Edward F., 71.
Stott, Charles A., 76.
Wright, Nathaniel, 42, 43.

ALDERMEN.

A.

Adams, John R., 40, 41.
Aiken, John, 37, 41.
Alger, Edwin A., 58, 62, 63.
Allen, Otis, 63.
Ames, Seth, 36, 37, 40.
Ashworth, Sager, 61.
Austin, William, 36.

Ayer, Frederick, 71.
Ayer, James H. B., 49, 50.

B.

Bancroft, Jefferson, 41, 42.
Bancroft, Selwin, 44, 45, 46.
Battles, Frank F., 70, 71.
Beard, A. Ithamar, 42.

Bedlow, Joseph, 40, 49, 50, 52.
Belden, Charles F., 76.
Blanchard, C. F., 54.
Brackett, Shadrach R., 55.
Bragdon, George, 47.
Brooks, Artemas L., 49, 55.
Brown, Darius C., 59.
Brown, Joseph S., 74, 75.
Brown, Samuel A., 66.
Brown, William, 65.
Brownell, George, 38, 49.
Bryant, Mertoun C., 62.
Bullens, Joseph M., 52, 53.
Burbank, Samuel, 52, 56.
Burke, William A., 62, 63.
Butterfield, Joseph, 46, 47.
Buttrick, Abner W., 67.

C.

Carleton, George H., 38, 39, 41.
Carll, Francis, 76.
Carter, Daniel, 49.
Caswell, Alonzo F., 74.
Chase, Samuel A., 75.
Chellis, Seth, 37, 38, 41.
Cheney, George S., 69.
Child, Linus, 47.
Clark, John, 39.
Coburn, Charles B., 56, 67, 68.
Coburn, Joseph B. V., 52, 53, 54.
Conant, O. J., 56.
Converse, Joshua, 51, 59.
Cooper, Isaac, 46.
Crombie, Daniel D., 49, 50.
Crowley, Jeremiah, 73, 74.
Cumnock, Alexander G., 72.
Cutler, Lucius A., 51.

D.

Dalton, John C., 45, 46.
Dana, David, 48.
Dobbins, William, 73.
Dodge, Charles W., 66.
Dodge, Joseph M., 58.
Douglas, Erastus, 48.
Dudley, Albion J. 66, 67, 68.

F.

Farr, Alpha B., 72, 73.
Farrington, Isaac, 73.
Fenno, James, 47.
Fiske, William, 51, 52, 55.
Fletcher, Horatio, 54.
Folsom, Jonathan P., 59, 61, 62, 73.
Francis, James B., 49, 50, 62, 63, 64.
French, Amos B., 70, 71.
French, Benjamin F., 38, 39.
French, Cyril, 41, 42, 43, 49.
Frost, Abner, 55, 60.
Frye, Frederick, 68.

G.

Gardner, William S., 60, 61.
Gates, Josiah, 65, 66.
Gerry, Gustavus A., 72.
Goodwin, John A., 75, 76.
Gove, Dana B., 64, 65.
Graves, Jacob, 48.
Graves, John W., 42.
Gray, William C., 46.
Green, John O., 39.
Griffin, Joseph, 43, 44.

H.

Haggett, Albert A., 71, 76.
Hardy, Philip, 50, 51.
Hildreth, Charles L., 68, 69, 70.
Hildreth, Henry A., 76.
Hill, Paul, 59.
Hooke, Henry M., 66.
Hosford, Hocum, 61, 67.
Howe, Henry C., 71, 72.
Howe, John F., 59.
Howe, Lorenzo G., 55, 59, 60.
Hubbard, John Q. A., 69, 70.
Huntington, Elisha, 47, 53, 54.
Huntoon, George L., 74.
Hutchinson, Samuel K., 53, 54.

J.

Jewett, Francis, 68, 69.
Jewett, Jeremiah P., 58.
Johnson, Henry C., 43.
Johnson, Jonathan, 56, 57.
Johnston, William S., 55.

K.

Kelley, William, 72.
Kendall, Jonathan, 74.
Kittredge, Joseph G., 37.
Knapp, Daniel, 45, 46.

L.

Ladd, Jonathan, 59.
Latham, Cyrus H., 64, 65, 69.
Lawrence, Ambrose, 51, 59.
Livingston, William, 42.
Livingston, William E., 67, 68.

M.

Mack, Sewall G., 47, 58.
Manahan, Samuel T., 59, 60, 61.
Mansur, Aaron, 36.
Mansur, Stephen, 40, 47, 53.
McNeill, William T., 64, 65.
Mixer, John, 50.
Morse, William G., 60, 61.

N.

Nesmith, John, 57.
Newman, William, 48.
Nichols, Gilman N., 48.
Nichols, William, 63.
Norris, George W., 64, 65.
North, Frederick T., 72.
North, William, 51, 52.
Nourse, Francis H., 57.
Nute, Andrew T., 55, 57.

O.

Owen, James, 75.

P.

Parker, William H., 67.
Patch, Benjamin, 72.
Peabody, Josiah G., 50.
Pevey, Abiel, 58, 63.
Pevey, John M., 68.
Pillsbury, Harlin, 40, 43.
Plimpton, Albert B., 66.
Putnam, Addison, 70, 71.

R.

Rand, James H., 56.

Rice, Edward C., 67, 68.
Richardson, Alden B., 75.
Richardson, Daniel S., 48.
Richardson, George F., 64.
Rogers, Jacob, 75, 76.
Rolfe, Abiel, 51.
Runels, George, 64, 73.

S.

Salmon, William F., 71.
Sanborn, Nathaniel C., 74.
Sargent, Joseph L., 66, 67.
Sawtell, Josiah, 47, 48.
Sawyer, Jacob H., 73.
Scripture, Isaac F., 62, 63.
Sherman, Edward F., 70.
Silver, Harvey, 58.
Smith, Henry, 44, 45, 46.
Smith, John W., 71.
Smothers, Jonathan, 57.
Southwick, John R., 66, 67.
Southworth, William S., 64.
Spalding, Ira, 53, 54.
Spaulding, Sidney, 43.
Sperry, Charles, 54.
Stanley, George E., 76.
Stevens, Alpha, 52, 53.
Stevens, George, 73, 74.
Stickney, Samuel W., 57, 58.
Stott, Charles A., 69, 70.
Swan, Charles A. F., 73.
Swan, Joshua, 37.

T.

Tapley, Joseph, 36.
Thurston, Nathaniel, 42.
Tilden, Charles L., 38, 39, 43.
Townsend, James, 50, 51.
Tuck, Edward, 56, 59, 73.
Tuttle, John B., 57.
Tyler, Jonathan, 40.
Tyler, Silas, Jr., 68.

V.

Varney, Samuel J., 52, 59.

W.

Waite, Aldis L., 61, 62.

Walker, Benjamin, 36.
Walker, Benjamin, 72, 74, 75.
Watson, Edward F., 44, 45, 60, 65.
Watson, James, 60, 61.
Webster, William P., 56.
Wheeler, Albert, 58, 62, 63.
Whipple, Oliver M., 36, 38, 39, 44, 45, 48.
White, Joseph, 53, 54.

Whitney, David, 61.
Wiggin, William H., 76.
Wilder, Charles H., 56.
Wilder, Henry H., 60, 65, 69.
Woodward, Daniel, 55.
Woodward, John C., 57.
Wright, Alexander, 36, 37.
Wright, Hapgood, 56, 69, 70, 75.
Wright, John, 44.

COMMON COUNCIL.

A.

Abbott, Joel A., 74, 75.
Abbott, Joshua, 37.
Adams, Joel, 47.
Adams, Jonathan, 45.
Adams, Sylvanus, 40.
Aiken, John, 49.
Allen, Nathan, 57.
Allen, Otis, 43, 48.
Allen, Otis L., 47, 48.
Anderson, William H., 68, 69.
Appleton, Isaac, 42.
Atherton, Abel T., 71, 72.
Avery, John, 48.
Avery, John, 2d, 58.
Ayer, Abel M., 61.
Ayer, James C., 63.

B.

Bachelder, David S., 47.
Badger, George W., 68, 69.
Baker, William, 37, 38.
Balch, Daniel, 45, 46.
Bancroft, Jefferson, 39, 40.
Barnard, William, 58, 59.
Baron, Jacob, 61, 66.
Bartlett, Stephen, 55.
Bass, William, 73.
Battles, Cyrus, 43.
Battles, Joseph, 40.
Baxter, Henry J., 36, 38, 39, 43.
Beck, Samuel, 61.
Belden, Charles F., 72, 73.
Bennett, James W., 76.
Bennett, John, 55.

Bird, Andrew, 37.
Bixby, Daniel, 43.
Blake, Jesse, 58, 59.
Blanchard, Amos A., 71, 72.
Blanchard, C. F., 53.
Blanchard, William D., 59, 61.
Blood, Andrew, 58.
Blood, Orford R., 75, 76.
Bohonan, Morrill M., 60, 61.
Bonney, Milton, 52, 53.
Bowers, Francis H., 41.
Bowers, Jonathan, 36, 46.
Bowers, Jonathan, 53, 54.
Boyden, Erastus, 57, 58.
Brabrook, Joseph A., 58.
Bradley, William H., 54.
Bradt, David, 43, 44.
Bradt, Garritt J., 38, 39.
Brady, Frank, 73, 74.
Bragdon, George, 41.
Bragg, Maynard, 49, 50, 55.
Brigham, Danforth P., 45, 46.
Brown, Darius C., 51, 52, 54.
Brown, Eliphalet, 38, 39.
Brown, Francis, 68, 69.
Brown, Joseph S., 72, 73.
Brown, Leonard, 53, 54, 58, 59, 71, 72.
Brown, Samuel W., 40, 41, 47.
Brown, Willard, 43.
Brown, Willard A., 69, 70.
Brown, William, 45, 46.
Brownell, George, 36, 37.
Bumpus, George G., 53.
Burbank, Samuel, 40, 41.
Burgess, Ebenezer, 58, 59.
Burgess, Horatio G., 62.

Burgess, Thomas F., 66, 67.
Burnap, Ethan, 40, 41.
Burnham, Crawford, 71, 72.
Butcher, Robert H., 66, 73.
Butler, Josiah, 75.
Butterworth, Benjamin S., 58, 59.
Buttrick, Abner W., 40, 44, 45, 50.
Buttrick, Alden B., 56.

C.

Callahan, Charles, 76.
Carleton, Stephen, 39.
Carll, Francis, 75.
Carlton, William, 42, 43.
Carolin, Thomas, 74, 75.
Carpenter, Benedict O., 62, 63.
Carroll, Henry H., 56, 57.
Carter, Henry P., 69, 70.
Caswell, Alonzo F., 72, 73.
Caswell, Michael B., 52, 53.
Cater, Joseph, 61.
Caverley, Zachariah B., 51, 52.
Chandler, Francis H., 71.
Chase, Alfred H., 66, 67, 68.
Chase, John K., 56.
Chase, Samuel M., 72, 73.
Cheney, Cleveland J., 62, 64.
Cheney, George S., 67, 68.
Child, Linus, 51.
Choate, George, 44, 45.
Church, Henry C., 71.
Churchill, Daniel, 64.
Clark, John, 36, 44.
Clark, Jeremiah, 52.
Clough, Henry P., 60, 61.
Coburn, Charles B., 44, 51.
Coburn, Fordyce, 50, 51, 63.
Coburn, Stephen A., 47.
Collins, David M., 56.
Conihe, William, 47, 48.
Conlan, Patrick, 53, 54.
Converse, Joshua, 40.
Cook, Mark H., 55.
Cook, James, 36, 53.
Cooper, Eli, 38.
Cooper, Isaac H., 41.
Corbett, Michael, 70, 71.
Corliss, Horatio G. F., 44, 46, 59.

Cosgrove, John, 63, 64.
Cowley, Charles, 75, 76.
Crane, Charles T., 68.
Crane, John J., 40, 41.
Critchett, Nathaniel, 41, 42, 48.
Crombie, James C., 47, 48.
Crosby, Caleb, 49, 50, 57, 59, 60.
Crowley, Jeremiah, 70, 71.
Cummiskey, Hugh, 43, 44.
Cummiskey, Patrick, 70, 71.
Currier, Jeremiah M., 48, 49.

D.

Dana, David, 36, 38.
Dana, George E., 61.
Dane, George, 40.
Dane, Osgood, 37.
Daniels, Joshua W., 55.
Davis, Elisha, 49.
Davis, Samuel G., 47.
Dean, Benjamin C., 76.
Decatur, Joseph, 49.
Dennis, Edward P., 75.
Dennis, Richard, 51.
Dickey, Hanover, 58.
Dinsmoor, James, 49.
Dobbins, William, 67, 71.
Dodge, Charles W., 64, 65.
Dodge, Joseph M., 37.
Dodge, Luke C., 65, 66.
Donovan, Matthew, 70.
Douglass, Erastus, 36, 38.
Douglass, Roswell, 42.
Downs, John E., 63, 64.
Downs, Rollin C., 62, 66.
Dudley, Albion J., 62, 63, 64.
Dudley, Willard, 58.
Durgin, John H., Jr., 69, 70, 71.

E.

Eames, Luther J., 72.
Eastman, Charles J., 74.
Eastman, Charles S., 54.
Eaton, Forrest, 39, 40, 44.
Ela, Horace, 71, 72.
Elliott, George P., 50, 51.
Emerson, Solomon D., 51.

F.

Farr, Alpha B., 58, 69, 70.
Farrington, Isaac, 46, 47.
Farrington, Southwell, 72.
Farrington, Willis, 76.
Favor, Nathaniel B., 49, 50.
Favor, Nathaniel P., 72, 73.
Fay, Samuel, Jr., 45.
Fellows, James K., 37, 56.
Fenno, James, 45.
Fielding, Josiah B., 60.
Fielding, Stephen K., 55.
Fifield, Edward, 51, 52, 62.
Fisher, Waldo A., 49.
Fiske, William, 37, 38, 41, 50.
Fiske, William O., 69, 70.
Fitts, Isaac N., 42.
Fitts, John L., 39, 40, 46.
Flagg, William H., 48, 49.
Flanders, Peter, Jr., 56.
Fletcher, Edmund D., 62, 63.
Fletcher, Horatio, 47.
Fletcher, William, 46.
Folsom, Alanson, 55.
Folsom, Jonathan P., 56, 67.
Foot, James L., 38.
Ford, John N., 51.
Foster, Amos H., 60.
Foster, James, 65, 67.
Frawley, Peter O'C., 54.
French, Abram, 52, 53.
French, Cyril, 36.
French, Everett W., 62, 63.
French, Josiah B., 36, 42.
Frye, Frederick, 62, 63.
Frye, Nathan W., 72, 73, 74.
Fuller, Jason, 74, 75.
Fuller, Perez, 38.

G.

Gage, Benjamin H., 37.
Gage, Seth, 56.
Gage, William H., 54.
Gale, Gilman, 44, 45.
Gardner, George, 50, 51.
Garity, Thomas R., 75.
Garland, Samuel, 36.
Garrett, Robert J., 57.

Gates, Elihu, 47, 48.
Gates, Josiah, 63.
Gerrish, Benjamin J., 43.
Gerrish, Thomas G., 64.
Gerry, Gustavus A., 65, 66, 67.
Gilman, Alfred, 43, 48, 49, 55.
Goddard, Benjamin, 50, 51.
Goddard, Charles T. 71, 74.
Goodale, William, 57, 59.
Goodspeed, Calvin, 38.
Googins, Benjamin L., 65, 66.
Goward, Zephaniah, 58.
Grady, William H., 76.
Gray, William C., 44, 45.
Greenhalge, Frederick T., 68, 69.
Grush, Joseph S., 53, 54.

H.

Hadley, John, 42.
Haggett, Albert A., 68, 69, 70, 73, 75.
Hale, Perley, 38.
Hall, Asa, 40.
Hallowell, Charles E., 76.
Hanson, Charles H., 76.
Hard, Charles F., 62, 63.
Harris, George L., 55.
Hartwell, James D., 70, 75.
Harvey, Charles H., 74, 75.
Hastings, Horatio W., 36.
Haviland, Francis N. J., 71.
Healey, David, 44.
Hill, Epaphras A., 69, 70.
Hill, Paul, 52, 54.
Hills, Eliphalet, 56.
Hilton, Hoyt W., 64.
Hinckley, Isaac, 56.
Hobson, George, 59, 60.
Hodge, William A., 66.
Holden, Benjamin F., 43.
Holland, John W., 41.
Holt, Joseph S., 39.
Holton, Frederick, 56, 57.
Hopkins, James, 42.
Hopkinson, Thomas, 38, 39, 48.
Horn, Samuel, 39.
Hosford, Hocum, 60, 70.
Hovey, William, 52.
Howard, Horace, 36, 38, 48.

Howard, John F., 75, 76.
Howe, Henry C., 53, 54.
Howe, James M., 57, 59.
Howe, John F., 57, 58.
Howe, Lorenzo G., 62.
Hubbard, Charles, 57, 64, 65.
Hubbard, Columbus J., 46.
Hubbard, John Q. A., 67, 68.
Hunt, John B., 67, 68.
Hunt, Jonathan T. P., 37.
Huntington, Elisha, 37, 38.
Huntoon, George L., 66, 67.
Hurd, Daniel, 55.
Hurd, George W. S., 73, 74.
Huse, Jesse, 47, 48, 49.
Hutchinson, R. M., 40.
Hutchinson, Thos. S., 46.
Hyde, Amos, 45, 46.

I.

Ireson, Benjamin S., 60.

J.

Jaquith, Leonard W., 52.
Jepson, John C., 57.
Jewell, Leonard F., 56.
Jewett, Andrew F., 64, 65, 66.
Jewett, Francis, 64, 65.
Jewett, Frank E., 61, 62.
Jewett, Jeremiah P., 42.
Jockow, Julius C., 71, 72, 74.
Johnson, Edward C., 47, 48.
Johnson, Jonathan, 55, 66.
Jones, George W., 51.
Jones, Phineas, 69, 70.
Jones, Stephen H., 76.
Jordan, True P., 72.

K.

Kelley, William, 68, 69.
Kendall, Jonathan, 42, 44, 52.
Kent, James, 65.
Keyes, Joseph B., 61, 62.
Keyes, Julian V., 65, 66.
Keyes, Patrick, 69, 70.
Kimball, Charles A., 66.
Kimball, Charles H., 76.
Kimball, Daniel R., 50.

Kimball, John F., 76.
Kimball, Jonathan, 57.
King, Gardner W., 76.
Kingsley, Enos O., 56.
Kittredge, Joseph G., 40.
Kittredge, William, 67, 69, 70.
Knapp, Daniel, 39, 40.
Knapp, Joel, 71.

L.

Ladd, Samuel G., 70, 71.
Lamson, Edwin, 68, 69.
Lamson, Tobias L. P., 64, 65.
Lamson, William, J., 49, 50.
Lamson, William H., 60.
Lancaster, Samuel T., 60, 61.
Latham, Cyrus H., 63.
Lawrence, Ambrose, 49.
Lawrence, Samuel, 2d, 50.
Lawton, James, 67, 68.
Lawton, Pliny, 43.
Leavitt, Erasmus D., 41, 42.
Lee, John T., 66, 67.
Lennon, Thomas, 54.
Livingston, Elbridge, 52.
Livingston, William, 41.
Locke, John G., 39.
Lord, Henry A., 72, 73.
Loughlin, James A., 73, 74.
Lyford, John B., 74, 75.
Lyford, Simeon G., 69, 70.
Lynch, Patrick, 71.

M.

Mack, Sewall G., 43, 44.
Mallard, Albert, 50, 51, 62.
Manahan, Samuel T., 58.
Manning, Daniel W., 76.
Mansur, Joseph W., 42.
Mansur, Stephen, 36, 39.
March, Oliver, 42, 43.
Marin, Samuel P., 74.
Maxfield, Jared P., 73, 74.
Maynard, John M., 58.
McAlvin, John B., 43, 45.
McCann, John, 63.
McEvoy, Hugh, 63.
McIntire, Lewis, 39.

McNeill, William T., 62.
Mead, Franklin. 46, 47.
Mead, John, 42, 43.
Meadowcroft, John L., 70, 71.
Melvin, Abram T., 49.
Merriam, Amos, 44.
Merrill, John F., 68.
Merrill, Joshua, 50.
Minot, Willard, 52.
Mitchell, Chatles F., 43.
Mixer, John, 36, 38.
Moar, Stephen, 51.
Moody, David J., 46.
Moore, James M., 55, 65.
Morey, George F., 60, 61.
Morrison, James G., 61, 64.
Morrison, John, 41, 42.
Morse, Isaac S., 49.
Morse, Isaiah, 47.
Morse, Luther B., 59.
Morse, William G., 55, 57.
Morse, W. W., 49.
Moulton, John L., 70, 71.
Munn, Francis D., 68, 69.

N.

Nesmith, John, 39, 40, 42, 48.
Nesmith, Thomas, 36, 37.
Newman, William, 47.
Nichols, Alanson, 57.
Nichols, David, 59.
Nichols, Gilman N., 44, 45, 46.
Nichols, William, 57, 58, 60.
Norris, George W., 61, 62.
North, Frederick T., 65, 66, 67.
North, William, 37.
North, William L., 61.
Nourse, David, 36.
Nourse, Francis H., 55, 56.
Nowell, Foster, 60, 61, 67.

O.

Orange, Henry S., 61, 62, 63, 68.
Ordway, Thomas, 36.
Osgood, Ben, 43, 44.
Osgood, George N., 65.
Osgood, Josiah, 37, 40.
Osterhordt, Simeon D., 65.
Owens, James, 73, 74.

P.

Packard, Lewis, 46.
Page, Isaac, 58.
Page, Jonathan, 50.
Parker, Isaac N., 47, 48.
Parker, William C., 52, 53.
Parker, William H., 61.
Parmenter, Horace, 48.
Partridge, George W., 59, 60.
Patch, Benjamin, 69, 70.
Patch, Henry, 40, 41.
Patten, Joseph A., 55, 68, 69.
Patterson, George W., 52, 53.
Patterson, James, 42, 43.
Paul, George K., 55.
Paul, Rufus, 38.
Payne, Edward J., 42, 43.
Peabody, Josiah G., 59, 60.
Pearson, John, 65.
Perkins, Henry P., 60, 61, 70, 71, 72.
Perkins, M. Gilbert, 61, 67, 76.
Perkins, Paul, 52, 53.
Perrin, Lewis L., 64, 65.
Pettingell, John, 62.
Pevey, Abiel, 56, 57.
Phelps, Jesse, 37, 38.
Philbrick, Calvin, 53, 54.
Pickering, Samuel K., 53, 54.
Pickman, John J., 76.
Pierce, John N., jr., 67, 68.
Pillsbury, Harlin, 39.
Pinkham, George E., 69.
Pinkham, James N., 66.
Place, Isaac, 56.
Pollard, Joseph S., 64, 65.
Pooler, Seth, 52.
Potter, William, 41.
Powers, Hannibal, 47, 48.
Powers, Joel, 46, 47.
Powers, Peter, 56.
Prescott, Samuel D., 67, 68.
Puffer Asahel D., 59.
Putnam, Addison, 64.

Q.

Quimby, Enoch, 60.
Quinn, John, 62, 63.

R.

Rand, James H., 58.
Rand, Oliver P., 55.
Randlett, Thomas L., 38, 39.
Read, Elijah M., 37.
Read, William A., 75, 76.
Reed, Edward E., 74, 75.
Reed, Ransom, 48.
Rice, Edward C., 65, 66.
Richardson, Daniel S., 45, 46.
Richardson, George F., 62, 63.
Richardson, Julian A., 74.
Richardson, William A., 49, 53, 54.
Ripley, George, 64, 65.
Robbins, Jacob, 39.
Roby, Augustus B., 55.
Rodliff, Ferdinand, 40.
Rogers, David, 56, 57.
Rogers, Rufus, 52, 53.
Rogers, Zadock, 46.
Rolfe, Abiel, 48, 56.
Rugg, Chester W., 65, 66.
Runels, Charles, 76.
Runels, George, 62.
Russell, Alonzo L., 72.
Russell, James, 36, 37, 42, 44.

S.

Salmon, William F., 58, 59, 60.
Sanborn, Amos, 69.
Sanborn, Edwin, 76.
Sanborn, Elon A., 61, 62.
Sanborn, Nathaniel C., 71, 72, 73.
Sands, James, 56.
Sargeant, Benjamin C., 51, 52, 56, 57, 58.
Sargent, Joseph L., 60, 61.
Sargent, Stephen P., 50, 51.
Saunders, Alfred S., 49, 60, 61.
Saunders, Charles W., 63.
Savels, John A., 36.
Sawtell, Calvin, 67, 68.
Sawtell, George F., 63.
Sawtell, Josiah, 45, 46.
Sawyer, Jacob H., 74.
Scott, Alfred, 66, 67.
Scott, John, 74.
Scribner, George F., 57.

Scripture, Isaac, 44, 45.
Seavey, Josiah, 42.
Shedd, Varnum A., 42.
Shepard, John, 67, 68.
Shepard, William, 72.
Sherman, Aaron H., 38.
Sherman, Edward, 45.
Sherman, William W., 64.
Short, Charles M., 46, 47, 48.
Simonds, John P., 43, 44, 45.
Skillings, David G., 70.
Sleeper, Charles W., 75.
Slocum, John P., 60.
Smiley, Stephen J., 73, 74.
Smith, George, 73.
Smith, John, 41.
Smith, John C., 52, 53, 54.
Smith, John W., 49, 50.
Smith, Oliver W., 66.
Smothers, Jonathan, 50, 51.
Southwick, John R., 47, 65.
Southwick, Royal, 41.
Spalding, Ira, 42, 43.
Spalding, Sidney, 36.
Spalding, Weld, 36.
Spencer, Ethan N., 68.
Sprague, Levi, 59, 64.
Stacey, Lucian P., 55, 69, 70.
Stafford, William, 63.
Stanley, George W., 53, 54.
Stanley, Stephen T., 57.
Starbird, Charles D., 76.
Stearns, Nathaniel, 63.
Stevens, Solon, 46, 47.
Stickney, Daniel, 73, 74.
Stiles, Lewis, 76.
Stockman, Edward, 75, 76.
Stott, Charles A., 59, 60.
Stott, John, 70, 71.
Straw, Levi H., 54, 55.
Streeter, Holland, 51, 52, 56.
Sweetser, Theodore H., 51.

T.

Talbot, Julian, 72.
Tapley, Joseph, 37.
Taylor, Amos A., 54.
Taylor, Ivers, 49, 50.

Thissell, Earl A., 72, 73, 75.
Thomas, Marcus A., 53, 54.
Thompson, Marshall E., 56.
Tilbetts, Temple, 57.
Tilton, Abram, 37.
Tilton, Charles F., 72, 73.
Tilton, George W., 74, 75.
Townsend, James, 42.
Tripp, John, 50.
Tripp, John L., 43, 44.
Tuck, Edward, 58.
Tukey, Frederick S., 64.
Twichell, William, 51, 52.
Tyler, Artemas S., 73.
Tyler, Ignatius, 47, 48.
Tyler, Jonathan, 36, 39.
Tyler, Joseph, 37.
Tyler, Silas, Jr., 67.

U.
Upham, William, 38.

V.
Varney, Samuel J., 50, 51.
Varnum, Leavitt R. J., 75, 76.
Vinall, William D., 57.

W.
Walker, Benjamin, 38, 39, 40.
Walker, Benjamin, 65, 66, 71.
Walker, Charles H., 76.
Walker, Ruel J., 67, 68.
Walker, William, 68, 69.
Ward, Sullivan L., 60, 61.
Warren, Pelham, W., 40.
Warren, Theodore, 55.
Watson, Alden B., 64, 65.
Watson, Edward F., 40, 41.
Watson, James, 50, 51.
Weaver, Caleb G., 52, 53.
Webb, John E., 58, 59, 72, 73.
Webster, William P., 54, 58, 59.
Welch, Arnold, 41.
Welch, Charles A., 57, 74, 75.
Welch, John W., 75, 76.
Welch, Willard C., 45, 46.

Wentworth, Tappan, 36, 37, 39, 40, 41
Wentworth, Thomas, 47, 48.
Wetherbee, Asa, 44, 45.
Wheeler, Albert, 56.
Wheelock, Andrus C., 49
White, Jonathan, 41.
Whiting, Phineas, 41, 52.
Whitmore, George H., 66.
Whitten, William T., 56.
Wiggin, William, H., 57.
Wilde, Benjamin, 38, 39.
Wilder, Charles H., 37, 44, 45.
Wilder, Henry H., 53, 54.
Wilkins, Charles, 58, 59.
Willoughby, Asa W., 42.
Willoughby, John, 59.
Wilson, Foster, 67.
Wilson, Gerry, 48, 49.
Wilson, Hubbard, 54, 62.
Wilson, Nathaniel, 41.
Winslow, Edward, 41.
Wood, Samuel N., 64.
Woods, Edward P., 73, 74.
Woods, George F., 53, 54.
Woodward, John C., 54, 55.
Worthen, George W., 50, 51.
Wright, Albert D., 75.
Wright, Amos D., 62, 63.
Wright, Atwell F., 63, 64, 73.
Wright, Ezekiel, 49.
Wright, George S., 49, 50.
Wright, Hapgood, 45, 46.
Wright, John, 44.
Wright, Lorenzo P., 45, 46.
Wright, Nathan M., 67.
Wright, Nathaniel, Jr., 44, 45.
Wright, Walter, 37, 38, 39, 43.
Wright, William A., 63, 66.
Wyman, William, 36.
Wyman, William W., 37.

Y.
Young, Aaron B., 55.
Young, Artemas S., 64.
Young, Enoch P., 58.
Young, George W., 59, 60.

PRESIDENTS OF THE COMMON COUNCIL.

Adams, Joel, 47.
Anderson, William H., 69.
Aiken, John, 49.
Chase, Alfred H., 68.
Clark, John, 36, 44.
Dean, Benjamin C., 76.*
Frye, Nathan W., 74.
Gardner, George, 51.
Gerry, Gustavus A., 66, 67.
Gilman, Alfred, 55.
Haggett, Albert A., 70, 73, 75.
Holton, Frederick, 57.
Hopkinson, Thomas, 39, 48.
Huntington, Elisha, 37, 38, 39.†
Kimball, John F., 76.

Mansur, Joseph W., 42.
March, Oliver, 43.
North, William L., 61.
Perkins, Henry P., 71, 72.
Richardson, Daniel S., 45, 46.
Richardson, William A., 53, 54.
Richardson, George F., 62, 63.
Ripley, George, 64, 65.
Salmon, William F., 60.
Sargeant, Benjamin C., 52, 56, 58.
Taylor, Ivers, 50.
Warren, Pelham W., 40.
Webster, William P., 59.
Wentworth, Tappan, 41.

* Resigned on removing from Lowell.
† Resigned to take the office of Mayor, made vacant by the death of Luther Lawrence.

CONTENTS.

	PAGES.
PREFATORY,	5– 15
MORNING PROGRAMME,	9
AFTERNOON PROGRAMME,	11
MR. FRYE'S ODE,	12
MR. CUDWORTH'S ADDRESS,	16– 26
MR. KIMBALL'S ADDRESS,	27– 31
DR. HUNTINGTON'S LETTER,	32
MR. COWLEY'S REMARKS,	33
MAYOR STOTT'S REMARKS,	34
DR. EDSON'S PRAYER,	35
GEN. BUTLER'S ORATION,	36– 50
MR. LOWELL'S ADDRESS,	51– 56
BISHOP CLARK'S ADDRESS,	57– 60
MR. WILDER'S REMARKS,	61– 62
DR. GREEN'S ADDRESS,	63– 70
DR. MINER'S ADDRESS,	70– 74
MR. COLBY'S POEM,	74– 80
JUDGE AMES' LETTER,	80– 82
JUDGE ABBOTT'S LETTER,	82– 85
MR. BATCHELDER'S LETTER,	85– 87
MR. BALL'S LETTER AND POEM,	87– 90
JUDGE CROSBY'S LETTER,	90– 92
MISS LARCOM'S LETTER,	93– 95
DR. MILES' LETTER,	95– 97
MR. WELD'S LETTER,	97– 99
MR. PURDY'S LETTER,	99–101
JUDGE RICHARDSON'S LETTER,	101–102
MR. DEAN'S LETTER,	102–104
MR. CURRIER'S LETTER,	104–105
MR. PAYNE'S LETTER,	105–106
MR. HANSON'S LETTER,	106–107

MR. LAWRENCE'S LETTER,	107–108
MR. KIMBALL'S LETTER,	108–111
DR. THAYER'S LETTER,	111
MR. ROBINSON'S LETTER,	111–112
MRS. ROBINSON'S LETTER,	112–115
MR. MANSFIELD'S LETTER,	115–117
MR. WINTHROP'S LETTER,	118
DR. PALFREY'S LETTER,	118
MR. TARBOX'S LETTER,	119
JUDGE HOAR'S LETTER,	120
SENATOR BOUTWELL'S LETTER,	120
COL. SAWTELL'S LETTER,	121
GOV. RICE'S LETTER,	121
GOV. WASHBURN'S LETTER,	122–124
COL. ADAMS' LETTER,	124
MR. HOVEY'S LETTER,	125
MR. CROWNINSHIELD'S LETTER,	126
MRS. FRENCH'S LETTER,	127
GOV. STRAW'S LETTER,	128
MR. WEBBER'S LETTER,	128
MR. COWLEY'S LETTER,	129
MR. LAWSON'S LETTER,	130–131
MR. McEVOY'S LETTER,	132–136
MR. ORDWAY'S POEM,	137–142
MR. WRIGHT'S LETTER,	143
COUNCILMAN COWLEY'S REMARKS,	144–146
CITY OFFICERS,	148–151

Printed in Dunstable, United Kingdom